ordinary people called to do extraordinary things

To my dear wife.

My best friend.

Thank you for being patient with me.

Thank you for inspiring me.

Thank you for loving me.

I can't wait to sit with you tomorrow morning…

ordinary people called to do extraordinary things

Firm Foundations

Text © 2018 by Ben Atkinson

All photographs © 2018 by Ben Atkinson (created via upslash.com & canva.com)

Cover Design: © Ben Atkinson

Holy Clubs Publishing (2018)

All rights reserved. No part of this book may be reproduced or transmitted in any form or by any means, electronic or mechanical, including photocopying, recording, or by any information storage without the consent of the Author, Ben Atkinson or B & N Enterprises LLC. (except by a reviewer who desires to quote brief passages in connection with a review for inclusion in a magazine, website, newspaper, podcast, or broadcast.)

All Scripture quotations, unless otherwise indicated, are taken from the New King James Version®. Copyright © 1982 by Thomas Nelson, Inc. Used by permission. All rights reserved. Biblegateway, (since 1993); retrieved January 2018 from https://www.biblegateway.com/

Library of Congress Control Number:

Includes index. ISBN: 978-0-9981529-6-7

Copyright © 2018 B & N Enterprises, LLC

TABLE OF CONTENTS

THE HOLY CLUBS MISSION 4

What RESULTS can you expect? 5

7 REASONS YOU CAN DO THIS! 6

OUR STORY… 7

WHAT IS OUR SECRET FORMULA? 8

OUR 4 UNIQUE CORE VALUES: 9

HOW DOES FRIM FOUNDATIONS WORK? 10

TESTIMONIES… 11

PREPARING & PLANNING….. 12

HOLY CLUBS EVANGELISM 13

SALVATION… 14

9 PRE-FOUNDATIONS (1-9) 15

THE FATHER DESIRES A FAMILY 16

JESUS DESIRE'S A BRIDE..22

SIN HAPPENED…...31

THE CROSS…. 38

NEW CREATION 46

OVERCOMING TEMPTATIONS 58

HUMILITY 63

PRAYER #talk2God #textingGod..74

THE 10 LIES OF HOLINESS 80

24 FIRM FOUNDATIONS (pg. 90-161) 88

BIBLIOGRAPHY 161

NOW WHAT? 162

THE HOLY CLUBS MISSION

Ben Atkinson - Author and Director of ©holyclubs.com

We believe you are an ordinary person who is called to do extraordinary things, and we want to help you get there. Our Mission is to give you the necessary tools to take charge of your personal spiritual journey and grow into the extraordinary person you're called to be.

Think of us as the friend that walks by your side, helping you to revive your heart, to overcome, and to reach your goals. How many times have you tried to "reset" your walk with God, but just couldn't seem to gain traction? How many times have to gone to a conference, or an amazing church service, and thought, "Today is the day I'm gonna get my life together"? Maybe you didn't know what to do next. We've got the plan for you.

Our 24 FOUNDATIONS are simple and easy to follow. Our practical sections will show you how easy it is to hear the voice of God. Our proven techniques will give you the necessary tools to implement what you are learning, unlocking your heart to follow after God.

We challenge you to do this for yourself. What if this is the tool that God uses to equip you to get over the obstacles, to set your heart before the Lord, to hear His voice and jump into the race He has set before you? You are called to walk holy today, and we want to help get you there.

Let's get started today, because you are an….

ordinary person called to do extraordinary things.

ordinary people called to do extraordinary things

What RESULTS can you expect?

24 practical assignments to help you:

HEAR God's voice.

GROW your prayer life.

OPEN your heart to God's love.

REVIVE your heart in the beauty of holiness.

OVERCOME the little nagging struggles.

FREELY "Go" and make disciples.

UNLOCK creative writing skills.

9 BONUS Pre-Foundations:

CLIMB to new heights

REVIVE your heart in truth.

CAST off burdens.

7 REASONS YOU CAN DO THIS!

Unlock #happyholiness…
God, The Father, is holy, and He invites you to be holy just like Him. Jesus, the happiest man alive, joyfully calls you to be holy just like Him. The Holy Spirit, the most powerful force in all creation, has a desire to help you walk holy. Holiness is not what you "have to do", it is what you "get to do"! God wants to take you on a joyful journey of change: a journey where you leave the pain of your past, rise up as a new creation, and walk with Jesus pure and free. We call this #happyholiness. I want to start you on that journey today.

If God is for you…..
If God is for you, Then God has a plan to prosper you. The One who Created you (your Heavenly Father) has a plan for you to succeed. He who began a good work in you is faithful to complete it (Phil. 1:6). Remember, if God is for you then who can stand against you? (Rom. 8:31)

This is Easy….
We've taken the time to put together 24 groups of easy-to-follow material, each one taking less than 30 minutes to complete. All you have to do is read, talk2God, write — and pray! If you just take the time to do this, your life will change. It really is that simple.

The first time I did this….
I needed a change in my life, but I just couldn't find the right tools. Then, one day, God taught me how to talk to Him by using my Bible, a pen, and some paper. After that, He taught me how easy it was to hear His voice. I was so excited! I finally had the tools I needed to grow my heart in #happyholiness #lifestyleofholiness.

He hasn't given up on you…..
God hasn't given up on you, so don't give up on yourself! The best is yet to come. Remember and be confident in this very promise, that He who has begun a good work in you will complete it until the day of Jesus Christ (Phil. 1:6).

You still have promises….
I know there is more for you. The Bible says there is more. Remember, all the promises of God in Him are Yes, and in Him Amen, to the glory of God through us (2 Cor. 1:20).

We went through the BIG books……
In this day and age you have crazy teachers who will tell you whatever you want to hear. We made sure this teaching was Jesus centered (we read the Bible and BIG books on: Jesus, Freedom, the Cross, and Purity). We did the hard work so that you don't have to. Let us take you on a journey to overcome.

ordinary people called to do extraordinary things

OUR STORY...

Why would I take time to write a Holy Clubs manual called "Firm Foundations" to lead you on the journey to #happyholiness? Well, it all started with a dream.

DREAM ABOUT HOLINESS

Years ago, I had a dream that I was a captain on a college track team. We were competing against other teams in the last meet of the year—the championship. After I finished my race, I was watching my team, but they were losing every single race and we were down 35-0. I knew that in tomorrow's news our team's loss would go up and down the east coast and all the others would know we were a weak team. My coach seriously asked me, "What are you going to do to encourage the team?"

I looked at my team, which was still running, and I got ready to fervently yell at the runners, encouraging them to win! But, despite my zealous cries, they did not win. Thankfully, we had one last race! So I got ready to rally the team, hoping we could win that last race. I turned to face the team, but everyone was gone. I asked my friend, "Where is the team?" He replied, telling me that they all left the race. They are not finishing the meet. Instead, they are standing in the tent, waiting for the buffet, which comes at the end of the meet.

I awoke and instantly knew what the dream meant:
The church has settled for a life of "just being saved"—they left their race of holiness—boringly waiting for the banquet at the end (The Wedding Supper of the Lamb; Rev. 19:9).

THE RACE: The track meet symbolizes the church's corporate race of holiness. We are supposed to walk holy & to "GO" make disciples. Your personal race of holiness affects the whole team.

35-0: We were losing 35-0 (Isaiah 35), which is a promise from God for Israel, declaring revival will come with power and miracles and GRACE to make His people Holy. Israel will walk on a highway of Holiness. Heb. 12:1-12 affirms that this truth is also valid for you today! God is calling you to run your personal race of holiness—by His GRACE! Your part affects the whole. But!

EVERYONE LEFT THE RACE: In the dream, everyone left the race, went to the tent, and waited for the buffet at the end of the event. The church in America is at a divine moment. We can either finish the race, or we can give up. You can either run your race of holiness or give up. PLEASE DON'T QUIT!!! Settling for "just being saved" and waiting to get into heaven, to eat at The Wedding Supper of the Lamb is not the end goal. Stay in the race of holiness and Go forth with God to make disciples. If you don't quit, you win!!! #happyholiness.

ordinary people called to do extraordinary things

WHAT IS OUR SECRET FORMULA?
We combined the WORD + SPIRIT = UNDERSTANDING

WORD: The Word of God is sacred (holy). The writer of Hebrews taught that God's Word was alive and active (Heb. 4:12). This means that His Word is truth that will transform you, and that it is the light to your path (Ps. 119:105) (today and in the age to come). The Word also reveals the heart, longing, and loving affections of God, teaching you who He is and what He thinks about you. We provide rich, biblically sound teachings, so that your soul will flourish in the safety of the Scriptures!

HOLY SPIRIT: The Spirit of God is a Counselor, Guide (John 16:13), Friend, and Teacher (John 14:26). Also, the Holy Spirit has creative power, bringing living and fresh revelation to your heart, soul, mind and strength (Eph. 1:17). The Holy Spirit searches the deep things of the Father (1 Cor. 2:10) and we provide the opportunity for you to enjoy and cultivate a fresh, vibrant, deep and loving relationship with Him.

UNDERSTANDING: **WORD + SPIRIT = UNDERSTANDING.** As you combine the Word (lamp) with the Spirit (guide) you will grow in Divine Understanding (powerful revelation). Divine Understanding is like a rushing, life-giving waterfall in your life. Imagine a river flowing along a stream bed, quickly picking up speed and then cascading over the edge, plummeting down, crashing upon the rocks below. The river bed is the Word, which provides firm foundations and boundaries, while the water is the Spirit of God, which flows along powerfully. The waterfall is the moment when the Word and the Spirit combine and LIFE explodes forth, taking everything from one level to the next! Holy Clubs provides the tools you need to go from one level to the next, so that Divine Understanding bursts forth, out of your innermost being like a waterfall of living water (John 3:8), touching even to the ends of the earth.

ordinary people called to do extraordinary things

OUR 4 UNIQUE CORE VALUES:

1. **Solutions not problems:** We focus on the solution and not the problem. Focusing on your problems only gets you more tired and more worn out. Searching out (and acting on) solutions inspires you to succeed.

2. **Inspired teaching about God's holiness:** We've created biblically sound teaching on Holiness. God graciously made a way for you to be holy — like Him! We give you the answers and invite you to walk towards them.

3. **Practical assignments called texting God:** We give you practical, engaging assignments called Texting God, which help you apply what you learned. These will revive your heart and train you to hear God's voice. It couldn't be any easier.

4. **Word and Spirit together:** We provide strong biblical content rooted and grounded in the Word of God. And we provide powerful moments of encounter with the Holy Spirit in the times of "Texting God", or when you "talk2God" during the personal prayer time. This abundantly helps build you up as a well-balanced person. Each lesson focuses on the solution, provides easy-to-follow biblical teachings, and follows up with practical assignments. We make it easy!

ordinary people called to do extraordinary things

HOW DOES FRIM FOUNDATIONS WORK?

9 Pre-Foundations (lessons take less than 30 minutes):

1. **READ:** 9 unique lessons for you to read that awaken your heart.

2. **WRITE:** quick and easy follow-up questions that reinforce TRUTH.

3. **PRAY:** we help you craft your own prayer for #happyholiness

24 Firm Foundations (lessons take less than 30 minutes):

1. **READ:** step-by-step training that teaches you "Firm Foundations" of the Faith.

2. **WRITE:** talk2God; our easy follow up steps invite you to "text God" and hear His Voice.

3. **PRAY: UP, IN, OUT** – we will teach to you pray the revelation God gives you right back to Him!

ordinary people called to do extraordinary things

TESTIMONIES….

"Last semester when I started going to Holy Clubs (Firm Foundations), I learned how precious our time with God is. I had been struggling with depression and suicidal thoughts this year. My thoughts were consumed with feeling purposeless, unwanted, and unloved. At one of our Holy Clubs, I had a huge breakthrough by "texting" God. **God spoke clearly into my life by telling me what life meant to Him". N. George – University student leader**

"Now, through the teaching in Holy Clubs (Firm Foundations), **I more intentionally spend time** in one or two verses asking who the Lord is, what He thinks about me, and praying that and agreeing with that." **Kelly Rogers – University student athlete**

"Ultimately, Holy Clubs (Firm Foundations) has been the place where I have **experienced God's personal love for me** the most, because it is a place that fosters personal encounter."
Tim McClaren – University student/prayer leader

ordinary people called to do extraordinary things

PREPARING & PLANNING.....

GO AT YOUR OWN PACE
In just 34 days time you are going to be a New Person (under 30 minutes each day).

9 DAYS TO COMPLETE <u>PRE-FOUNDATIONS</u> (instructions)

1. Mark off 9 days on the calendar.
2. Fill in the time of day you are going to complete each session.
3. Complete each session day-by-day.

24 DAYS TO COMPLETE <u>FIRM FOUNDATIONS</u> (instructions)

1. Mark off 24 days on the calendar.
2. Fill in the time of day you are going to complete each session.
3. Complete each session day-by-day.

"Only you can redeem the time the enemy has stolen from you, so let's PREPARE and PLAN for you to succeed" - Ben Atkinson (Author and Director of Holy Clubs)

ordinary people called to do extraordinary things

HOLY CLUBS EVANGELISM

Schedule a night of FUN, FOOD, & EVANGELISM.

All the Holy Clubs are encouraged to have a night of Fun, Food, and Evangelism. This is a time when you can invite new believers or someone that is not yet saved. Consider this as "group outreach". (Did you know that this is one of the most powerful ways to share the gospel with a friend, neighbor, or family member?) Then, afterwards, you can start a new Holy Clubs group with those that you are discipling. Amazing! It is that simple.

WHEN SHOULD YOU DO THIS?

I encourage people to host an outreach event after Firm Foundation #12, and before #13. (For no other reason then it is the halfway point.) But you choose whenever works best for your group.

RUN DOWN OF THE EVENT:

1. Set the Date.

2. Everyone bring a friend!

3. Everyone bring something to eat.

4. Have FUN! (Take time to do a fun group activity.)

5. Someone shares their testimony of when Jesus Saved them!

6. Share the Gospel of Jesus Christ: Take time to do a group presentation. Be creative! I encourage multiple people to take time to share different parts of the sheet **"DO YOU WANT TO START YOUR NEW LIFE WITH CHRIST?"**

***After people say "YES" to starting a relationship with Jesus, then take time to meet with your local church and ask about baptisms.

ordinary people called to do extraordinary things

SALVATION...
DO YOU WANT TO START YOUR NEW LIFE WITH CHRIST?

You can have powerful, personal, peace today through a relationship with Jesus Christ. Follow these steps one at a time and then pray the prayer at the end. The change will be in our heart.

Step 1 – The Father loves you. He desires a family!

The Bible says, "God so loved the world that He gave His one and only Son, Jesus Christ, that whoever believes in Him shall not perish, but have eternal life" (John 3:16). All you have to do is Believe in Jesus. Also, Jesus said, "I came that they may have life and have it abundantly"—a complete life, full of purpose (John 10:10). However, there is another important step...

Step 2 – People are sinful and our sin separates us from God.

We have all sinned. Each one of us have thought, said, or done something evil, which the Bible calls "sin". The Bible says, "All have sinned and fall short of the glory of God" (Romans 3:23). The wages (or debt) of our sin is death; the result of sin is our death; this is spiritual separation from God (Romans 6:23). But there is good news!

Step 3 – Our Heavenly Father sent His Son to pay the debt of your sin. He paid for our sins!

Jesus willingly died in our place so we could have a relationship with God and be with Him forever. "But God demonstrates His own love toward us, in that while we were still sinners, Christ died for us." (Romans 5:8) Thankfully, it didn't end with His death on the cross. The Father raised Christ from the dead, and Christ is the Kindest Man Alive! *"For I delivered to you first of all that which I also received: that Christ died for our sins according to the Scriptures, and that He was buried, and that He rose again the third day according to the Scriptures,"* (1 Corinthians 15:3-4). Therefore, Jesus is the only TRUE way to God. Jesus said, *"Jesus said to him, "I am the way, the truth, and the life. No one comes to the Father except through Me."* (John 14:6) Do you want this?

Step 4 – Would you like to receive God's forgiveness?

There is NO WAY to earn salvation; we are saved by God's grace when we BELIEVE (have faith) in His Son, Jesus Christ! All you have to do is confess that you are a sinner; confess that Christ died for your sins, and ask for His forgiveness. Then turn from your sins; this is repentance. Jesus Christ personally knows you and loves you. What really matters to Him is the attitude of your heart, your honesty, and sincerity (God can see into our heart and thoughts). I suggest praying the following prayer to start the continue the journey—accept Christ as your Savior TODAY!

Step 5 - Pray this prayer

My Heavenly Father "I confess that I'm a sinner, and I ask for your forgiveness.
I believe Jesus Christ is Your Son, and He is the Way, The Truth, and the LIFE. I believe that He died for my sin and that You raised Him back to life again.
I want to trust Him as my Savior and follow Him day-by-day as my Lord. Guide my life and help me to do your will. I pray this prayer in faith; wash my heart clean in your mercy and empower me through your grace. In Jesus' name I pray, Amen."

*If you just prayed this prayer, tell someone! Then email us at **holyclubs@gmail.com** and let us know that you just prayed the "SALVATION PRAYER".*

ordinary people called to do extraordinary things

GETTING STARTED....
9 PRE-FOUNDATIONS (1-9)

Day 1 - The Father desires a family

Day 2 - Jesus desires a Bride

Day 3 - Sin happened!!

Day 4 - The Cross

Day 5 - New Creation

Day 6 - Overcoming Temptations

Day 7 - God's Grace

Day 8 - Prayer

Day 9 - To be Holy

ordinary people called to do extraordinary things

THE FATHER DESIRES A FAMILY
Pre-Foundation #1

"For this reason I bow my knees to the Father of our Lord Jesus Christ, from whom the whole family in heaven and earth is named…" (Eph. 3:14-15)

GOAL

- **(Step #1)** To touch the heart of the FATHER.
- **(Step #2)** To live as a CHILD of God.

John, the beloved disciple, declares that you are called to be a son or daughter (child of God) and not a child of satan. "In this the children of God and the children of the devil are manifest: Whoever does not practice righteousness is not of God, nor is he who does not love his brother" (1 John 3:10).

But the Father loves you immensely and, "…is not slack concerning His promise, as some count slackness, but is long-suffering toward us, not willing that any should perish but that all should come to repentance" (2 Pt. 3:9). Therefore, He chases you down with unrelenting love. Remember, Jesus exposed to earth, Heavens' delight by sharing, *"I say to you that likewise there will be more joy in heaven over one sinner who repents than over ninety-nine just persons who need no repentance"* (Lu. 15:7).

The Father has an immeasurably strong desire for you to be in His family, and He gave up His only Son to adopt you (you are worth it). Wait … no, those words don't suffice. Let me try this again: the Father's desire for a family is stronger than the sun in all its glory! When was the last time you could stare at the sun for more than a moment? Even this analogy does not begin to scratch the surface of the Father's passion for Family. Revival is Family—God wants to spend eternity with you; He wants to be your eternal loving Father.

The Father affectionately made a promise to His Son about you being a part of the family. A foundational premise of God's kingdom is the Father's fundamental promise to give Jesus an inheritance: the Bride of Christ (Eph. 5:31-32; Rev. 19:7-9). Jesus longs for an eternal companion, a Bride, who voluntarily chooses to be equally yoked to Him in love. I know what you are thinking: how can I be the Bride? Am I gonna marry Jesus? Well, yes, but it might not be exactly in the way your thinking (Rev. 19:1-10). You will be married to Jesus without physically engaging with Jesus as a married couple does. (NOTE: Scripturally, the "sons of God" includes women, and the "Bride of Christ" includes men.)

An aspect of His inheritance involves the mandatory obedience of all creation (Rom. 14:10-12). Jesus desires you, and He desires to do the will of the Father—Revival is an Obedient Family. This immovable trust establishes you as a loved child of God the Father and a loved Bride of Christ—forever!

Imagine listening to the Father share about people to Jesus for the first time. I know Jesus is God, but the scripture declares you were hidden in Him before the foundation of the world (this is actually your adoption story; read this for further proof [Eph. 1:3-6]). You might ask, "what does that mean?" Genesis 1 sheds monumental light upon this.

In the beginning...wait, the beginning of what? Glad you asked. *"In the beginning God created the heavens and the earth. The earth was without form, and void; and darkness was on the face of the deep. And the Spirit of God was hovering over the face of the waters"* (Gen. 1:1-2).

Did you catch that one little phrase...The "earth was without form, and void." It was created, but was without form. When was the last time you created something, but it was without form? Actually, you do this a lot. Whenever you create a plan in your mind, the plan exists, but it is without form. Then once you actually execute the plan, it exists. So, there was a time when God created the Heavens and the Earth, but the earth was without form and void. This means it was still in the heart of the Father. There was a time you existed as the dream of the Father's heart before the foundation of the earth. Remember, He said to Jeremiah, *"Before I formed you in the womb—I knew you"* (Jeremiah 1:5). In the same way, He created you in His mind, and then shared you with Jesus.

But our story does not start there. You, my friend, must ask where? Where was God the Father when He created the Heavens and the Earth? Interesting questions aren't they? If you're like me, you always thought that The Father dwelt in Heaven, but the first Scripture of the Holy Word says that He "created Heaven." So where was He living before He created Heaven? The answer is (drum roll please...), hidden in a song from the 4 living creatures. They declare, *"Holy, holy, holy, Lord God Almighty, Who was and is and is to come!"* (Rev. 4:8). He is the God "who was". He "was" there in the Secret Place before the foundation of the world.

He existed in Perfectly Perfect Perfection—He was there where He was. Where was that? It is where the Father was. (Don't get mad at me, I am simply saying that where He is becomes Perfectly Perfect Perfection.) The four living creatures declare His Majesty while telling the story of His existence before the foundation of the World.

Imagine if you will that moment when the perfect Father first describes you to Jesus. Yes, describes you, because after all God created you, and He has great BIG plans for your future. (Why do you think the devil is trying to destroy your life? Because God has big plans for you.)

If Jesus knew Jeremiah before He actually formed him in the womb, then we can conclude He knew you before you were actually physically formed (Jer. 1:5). So, I'll ask the question again: Where were you before you physically existed? Remember, You were His perfect plan; you were the amazing dream in the heart of the Father.

Do you recall when He created Heaven and earth? Clearly, they both existed in His heart before they were created in the natural; after all, He is the most creative architect. (In the beginning God created the heavens and the earth, but the earth was "without form, and void." It was still in the heart of the Father. As the most skillfully detailed architect, He drew all and planned all ahead of time.) Likewise, you existed before He actually formed you in the womb. The Father knew you; He had a plan for you that lasted into eternity. The Father has a plan to enjoy you—Revival is Family—FOREVER.

So back to the question. What was the Father seriously thinking and feeling the first time the Father described you to Jesus? Seriously think about it. If you, the perfect Dream of the Father, existed in His heart, then when was the first moment that Jesus knew you? Was it before your mother's womb?

The book of Revelation gives us a massive amount of insight into this in one simple Scripture. Revelation 13:8 declares that, "Jesus is the Lamb slain from (or before) the foundation of the world." You should be shouting how remarkable this is. Truly, this is a most remarkable discovery of monumental degrees. This means that He saw you, He met you; He saw the Father's immeasurable LOVE for you. He saw that you are part of the Family of God. Unfortunately, He saw that your willful sin would keep you from Heaven's gate. He first loved you, therefore Jesus chose to sacrifice His life to be your Savior. He chose to be the Lamb that would be slain, before the foundation of the world, for the sake of LOVE.

Now hold on, I know what you are thinking: I am some crazy internet preacher that is going to bellow about aliens and conspiracy theories. Wrong! I want to talk to you about truth.

What is truth? Truth has three or more components. Firstly, it must be confirmed in the holy Word of God and agreed upon by credible biblical scholarship. (I have heard people twist the Bible to speak whatever hair brained idea they have.) Secondly, truth must be unquestionably inspired by the Holy Spirit. The Holy Spirit must bear witness within the heart of the speaker and the community they serve with. Thirdly, (there are more, but I will just stay at three), truth must be historically possible. When someone is sharing an idea, then it must either have actually happened, or be possible (with God all things are possible). Therefore, the truthful statement I have made is that **Jesus met you before the earth existed physically**.

So, now you know, my friend, what you did not know yesterday. The joyful Father held you as a tender dream in His heart. You were "in Him" before the earth was even created. You still don't believe me? Consider what divine revelation the Apostle Paul had, "Just as He chose us in Him before the foundation of the world, that we (you) should be holy and without blame before Him in love, having predestined us to adoption as sons by Jesus Christ to Himself, according to the good pleasure of His will" (Eph. 1:4-5).

You should be excitedly standing on your head laughing with joy. You were chosen in HIM! You existed in the heart of the Father as His Dream! You are the dream of the Father's heart, and not for what you accomplished. Instead, it's just because He first loved you!

He fashioned you to be holy and without blame, in love, predestined. (Don't get tripped up on this word. It means that God knows the end from the beginning, and He still gives us all the dignity of a choice). Again, He predestined you to be adopted, to be a part of His Family. You see, you are not just saved from something, you are rightly saved for something—Revival is Family.

So, in summary, the Father wants a family, and you are a very important part in "The Family." Also, you were the exquisite Dream of the Father, who loved you before you existed physically. Jesus, for the sake of Love (love for His Father and equal love for you) became your Savior. He chose to humble Himself to the lowest of lows, become a man, redeem you, and He rose up to sit in vibrant intercession for you to succeed (Rom. 8:34; Heb. 7:25).

ordinary people called to do extraordinary things

FATHER ASSIGNMENT: practical assignment…answer the questions accordingly.
GROUP QUESTION: discuss whichever question seems most important.

1. Read Luke 15. From Luke 15:7 what does this Scripture show about God the Father?

2. From Luke 15:7 what does this show about what God thinks and feels about you?

3. Do you believe that you are in God's family, and that you are a child of God?

4. According to Luke 15:20 God the Father has _____ towards you. As a child of God you have the right to be loved by God.

5. According to Luke 15:22 As a child of God you have the right to God's inheritance. Fill in the blanks from (Lu. 15:22): "But the father said to his servants, 'Bring out the best _____ (clothed in righteousness) and put it on him, and put a _____ on his hand (authority to work in the kingdom) and _____ on his feet ("Go" and share the gospel).

6. What is keeping you from receiving God's love?

7. Do you have to tell God your sorry? Write down whatever you need to ask forgiveness for, and then ask Him to forgive you.

8. **Pray this prayer to receive more of the Father.** "Father, I know that You love me with an immeasurable love. I know that You fashioned me in Your very heart. I know that I am the dream of Your heart. I know that You are _____ (summary from #2). I know that You think and feel I am _____ (summary from #3). I know that I am Your child. I know that I have the right to be loved by You and receive Your inheritance. Therefore, fill me with Your love and give me my inheritance. Let me love You and be loved by You. Amen."

ordinary people called to do extraordinary things

JESUS DESIRE'S A BRIDE
Pre-Foundation #2

"**The Kingdom of Heaven is like a certain king who arranged a marriage for his son, And sent out his servants to call those who were invited to the wedding; and they were not willing to come.**" (Matt. 22:2-3)

GOAL
- **(Step #1)** To understand the heart of THE BRIDEGROOM.
- **(Step #2)** To live as a REDEEMED BRIDE.

Jesus loves the Father and deliberately lays down His life for the Father's will to be done (Lu. 22:42). And the Father's will is to have a family that includes you. Also, Jesus longs to share His heavenly glory with you (John 17:22-24). This is not like sharing a meal together, nor is it as trivial as sharing a few million dollars. Instead, this is God the Father enjoying

God the Son, enjoying you, equally enjoying each other forever—Revival is Family—a glorious Family. (Interesting side note: Did you know that Jesus loves you with the same intensity that He loves His Father? (John 15:9)

What does the Heavenly Family look like? Deep in the heart of the Father, He desires children (you as a child of God forever). But did you know that deep in the heart of Jesus, He passionately desires a Bride? In fact, the beloved Bride of Christ (put your name in here) is the great prize of all the ages, for which Jesus patiently awaits (Rev. 19:7). The affections of the human heart are one of the most precious possessions to God (Eph. 1:18). Why? Because of God's tremendous love for you and your extravagant worth to Him. Jesus died to redeem you, and thus eagerly desires your affections—you move the heart of God. You were made for love; you were made to love God and be loved by Him (Matt. 22:37). The reason you were created and redeemed is to be loved and to love Jesus with all your heart. **Satan attacks your heart so that you will NOT fully love God. He viciously desires for you to live as a slave instead of Jesus' inheritance.** Wisdom cries out, "Keep your heart with all diligence, for out of it spring the issues of life" (Prov. 4:23). Today, rise up, believe in your heart that you immensely matter to Jesus.

You are a son or daughter—a child of God—and you are the Bride of Christ. God's ultimate eternal purpose for creation is to provide a family for Himself that includes faithful children for Himself (the Father) and an equally yoked Bride, the eternal companion for His Son (Jesus). The Holy Spirit's job is to joyfully share God's heart of Love with you while releasing measures of grace for you to walk fully obedient unto the Lord. Your job is to not just be the Bride, but also to be a Friend of the Bridegroom, just like John the Baptist (Jn. 3:29). John wholeheartedly loves God and prepared the way for Jesus to come by loving people out of their sinful lifestyle. You can do this by living like John: Holy and set apart unto God. I know what you're thinking, "Seriously, I can't live holy, and I don't want to wear camel skin, eat locust and honey, while screaming in the desert, 'REPENT!'" Hold on, just because you don't think you can live holy doesn't mean God can't make you holy. Magnificent and holy is His nature. He is holy, and that is the invitation for your life (1 Peter 1:16). You are made for greatness; you are an ordinary person called to do extraordinary things.

You may think, "I don't feel so amazing. So why do you think I was made for greatness?" Because God heartily promised to give Jesus an inheritance consisting of a people whom He fully possesses in love. *"I (the Father) will give You (Jesus) the nations for Your inheritance, and the ends of the earth for Your possession"* (Ps. 2:8). Still not convinced? Let's open up the Bible to Isaiah chapter 49 and peer into a conversation that happened a long time ago.

Imagine (and I say imagine because holy imagination is given to you by God) that you are a scribe in heaven (I am not sure how this would work, but just imagine for a brief moment). Ok, settle down and imagine that you are a scribe in Heaven, and it is your job to record the conversations that the Father has with the Son. So quickly grab your pen, spread out your holy parchment, and let's get ready to write—the Father is about to speak!

"Son?" the Father says with the tender ponderings of the Most Ancient of Days. When Wisdom ponders, you know the truths about to be revealed are truly Heavenly. Continuing the divine dialogue, He playfully asks, "Do you want to know what is on My heart?"

Jesus, majestically seated at the right hand of the Father, turns, and with an expectant and excited smile, remembering all the wonder and creativity that has burst forth each time this question has been previously asked, enthusiastically replies, "Amaze Me."

"As you know, I have created children—My sons and daughters—each one the very dreams of My heart," the Father says, while proudly looking at you, while looking at me, while looking at all of humanity, still hidden in the very depth of His heart. This is where you were before you existed physically. You are the dream of the Father's Heart. You are His inheritance. You are the joy of the Father, the one He wants to spend eternity with. Jesus, thinking upon these things, smiles with eager anticipation of the future. And then the divine Inventor of creativity stands and turns compassionately to His Son and prepares to speak.

Jesus notices a questioning dilemma arise upon the Father's face. Agonizingly, the Father says, "But!" This word causes bright lightning to explode from the Father in a circular ball of energy, followed by deafening thunder pounding the air like a shockwave. "Sin, the devil's twisted lies, will keep My children from Me. Sin will keep them from eternity with Me. Sin is robbing My family of true happiness." Jesus hears the words come out of His Father's mouth while hearing the stories within each word. It is your story and mine. What story? Imagine, for a moment, a book—not just any book, but a very special book penned by the Father. It is the story of your life, before you existed physically. After all, you are the dream within the heart of the Father. It is the book of your life, my life, your families' lives, and the lives of your neighbors. Now imagine that God has written a wonderful story filled with His precious thoughts towards you and your response. These books are made of three volumes:

1. **Volume 1: "The Dream of the Father"**

    This is your life while you're still hidden in the heart of the Father. He created you; He writes the story of your life and holds you as a dream within His heart; Jesus is introduced to you; Heaven is physically created; Earth will be physically created in 7 days.

2. **Volume 2: "This is your life"**

    After you're fashioned in your mother's womb, then you are born, and your life is unfolding day-by-day on Earth. This book records the conversations and intentions of the Father's desire for you to succeed and walk holy. Then, if you stumble and fall, Jesus is there to redeem you, and the Holy Spirit is there to fill your repentant heart with cleansing Mercy while empowering you to walk forth in Grace.

3. **Volume 3: "The Age to Come"**

    In the Age to Come, you will be enjoyed by the most magnanimous lovable Father, tenderly loved by Jesus the Bridegroom King, and wisely counseled by the loving Holy Spirit while loving your neighbor as yourself—forever.

At this moment, Jesus, who is the the Living Word of God, watches sin trying to erase the story of your life, while the Father loudly laments as sin seeks to destroy the dream (your story) which is perfectly safe in His heart. Sin, an outside force, not greater than God, but evil and deceitful in nature. It is there to rob, steal, kill, and destroy. It is there to separate you from God forever. Imagine the pain of a mother that has just had her child stolen out of her hands. Imagine the terrifying cry of grief that would explode out of her mouth as she wails for her lost child. Then multiply that measure of grief by 1 billion and you can barely begin to imagine the pain that the Father feels in having been separated, having you stolen by the horrible, wretched, lying deceiver, satan. The Father weeps, for sin has stolen you from His heart. The way the Father loves the Son is the same way God loves you.

Jesus marvels at the Father's immense love for you. (Side Note: Have you read the verse declaring the Father extravagant love? He loves you with the same love He has always had for Jesus ([John 15:9](#))? Jesus sees that sin would keep you from Him, from His love. Jesus sees there is no one who would come to your rescue. Jesus sees a court case: you against your sin. He sees that you would lose, as everyone loses this court case. He sees that you would be separated from the Father and His love forever. Jesus sees that the debt of sin is more than any human being could ever hope to pay back. Jesus sees there is no intercessor for you. He sees that the Father loves You immensely. He sees the pain of you being stolen, like a child out of the hands of a mother, by sin. Jesus sees that you would be separated from the Father forever.

Jesus looks at His Father, still fondly looking at you. Keep in mind: at this point, you do not exist yet physically. You are still just a dream in the heart of the Father, but very much alive —for the Great Architect, the Beginning and the End, has already created you; Jesus knew you before you were perfectly fashioned in your mother's womb. When sin comes...when violent sin comes to steal you away from the Father...when the dream of your eternal existence is being stolen away by a swindling thief and liar, aborted before you were born...at that moment, when the scales of justice seem to tip in favor of sinister, sinful satan, something happens that causes time to stand still, causing hope to arise, filling all Heaven with glory–!

Jesus, looking at the anguish of the Father as He was losing you, vows within His heart, "Yes." But, yes to what? Jesus, the Great Intercessor, steps forth and professes, "Father, I desire that Your sons and daughters, whom You love, would come home, that they would be with You where You are, for you loved me before the foundations of the World, and You love humanity as You love Me" ([John 17:24](#)). When He says this, He is actually agreeing with the Father's will, His plan from the beginning. The Lion would become the Lamb, laying down His God form to become a human (in comparison to you becoming a worm for the sake of saving worms). He says `yes` to vicious torture upon the cross that you might live. He says `yes` to standing in the gap for you. He chooses to pay the debt for your sin. Why? Because the Father first loved you ([1 John 4:19](#)). Jesus makes a way for you to love and be loved by the Father so that you, as a child of God, will feel the protective, providing, pastoral love of the Father forever. But this is not the only reason why Jesus steps forward to save you. There is another reason equally as compelling and deeply meaningful to Jesus: He is longing for a Bride.

Jesus, who is the Son of God and the Savior of all mankind, is also the Beloved Bridegroom ([John 3:29](#)), and you are called to be a Friend of the Bridegroom and prepare the Second Coming of the Lord. "Father," Jesus affirms, "I will go. I will go and be the Implanted Seed, the Word of God, sown into fertile ground for the harvest, where You gather Your Sons and Daughters" ([James 1:21](#)). The Father reaches out His hand and places it upon the back of Jesus' head. With a grateful smile and tender affection, He rejoices to say, "Go and love Your Bride, who will be taken by another. But within that will be a massive division. Redeem them, return, and wait for them to invite You to be their Savior, Bridegroom, King and Judge" ([Matt. 23:39](#)).

Jesus, in that moment, before earth existed physically, becomes manifest as the Bridegroom of all eternity. Not only is Jesus saving you from something, He is saving you for something. He is saving you to be loved by the Father and loved by the Bridegroom (in a non-sexual way). You, in all your weakness, in all your pain, both past and present, are loved by the Perfect Bridegroom, the One that left Heaven to come and get you. This is the greatest love story ever told. It is greater than any Hollywood story that has ever unfolded. The villain has stolen the girl, turned the girl against her lover, and he is seeking to destroy her and her offspring. However, the Hero (Jesus the Bridegroom) risks all for the sake of love to make the miraculous rescue. Jesus leaves Heaven to rescue you, the Bride of Christ, and He will gather you back again with Him in Heaven (you are worth so much more than you know). And you will be perfectly loved by Our Father and Perfectly loved by the Bridegroom—Jesus—forever.

"Father," Jesus tenderly asks, "What does it mean that there will be a division in My Bride"?

"I have created both Jew and Gentile. Unfortunately, because of sin, they will be divided." The Father shares a tale of two peoples, a story that is yet to unfold.

Jesus looks at The Father and asks, "Father, what is hidden in your heart?" Jesus had learned that the Father is the Great Storyteller of all the ages (there are many stories hidden in His heart yet to be told). So when the Father is telling a story, it is import to ask for more.

The Father, looking down, turning, and walking to His left, begins to share. He does not share because He has to. Instead He is sharing because He was asked. Walking and talking, He states, "You will leave Heaven as My Servant. You will go forth as a child in a mother's womb. And then I will empower you to bring Jacob (this is Israel) back to heaven, to restore and preserve Israel." Jesus lets that sink in for a moment by pondering the words, meditating within His heart, and then waiting for the right question to arise. And then it does.

"What will be the sign of this?" Jesus asks inquisitively. "What will be the sign of my coming?"

"I will put a star in the east that will shout to the gentile nations, and I will put a choir of angels that will sing to the shepherds of Israel," the Father triumphantly declares. As Jesus ponders the very Words of Wisdom from His Father's Master Plans, He comes to the next logical question.

"And the Gentiles?"

The Father looks at His Son as all proud Fathers do, proud that His Son is hanging on every word and going deeper into the story, proud that He is asking about His Plan.

Joyfully, the Father proclaims, "Son, You are glorious! You are amazing! I love You so much. Therefore, it is too small of a thing to just bring Jacob back. I have other children that I want to come home (remember Revival is Family)." At this, an explosion happens in heaven. But before the explosion, Heaven stands still. Everything stands still. (Everything, except for you. You have to write. Remember that you are the little scribe writing what the

Father is sharing to the Son.) With time standing still, Jesus looks at you and millions of Gentiles in His very heart, each a story yet to come forth. And glorious light explodes out of the heart of the Father, the glorious light of billions of Gentile souls—sons and daughters—bursting forth; each like a snowflake with its own unique, creative character, bursting forth with vibrant rainbow colors, individually singing a personal song of love and devotion to the Father. These are all the Gentiles, created—the dream of the Father—but yet to be born.

Then the Father states to Jesus, "It is too small of a thing that you should just redeem Israel. I will make you a Light to the Gentiles (Isa. 49:6-7). Sin, will try to divide the two, but I will send you as a covenant to walk in between the two, to hang upon the cross in between the two. I will send you as a covenant. And you will be the Prince of Peace. Your sacrifice, Your LOVE, will unite the Jew and Gentile. You will unite Heaven and Earth. Just like a man and woman unite to become one flesh, You will unite Jew and Gentile. You will unite Heaven and earth. You will make the two one (Eph. 2:15)." Jesus, feeling the weight of every word is now on His knees in an overwhelming display of submission to the Father's will.

Then the Father speaks again. "I have chosen to live in Jerusalem, to establish My Throne. I have set My Son on My Holy hill of Zion (Psa. 2), the King above every king. You will be the Bridegroom King."

At that, Jesus watched a scene unfolding before Him. It was a little movie screen, the Father sharing what the future would hold, the Day of all Glory. Jesus stood transfixed by the movie unfolding before Him (the high-speed resolution was out of this world). The Father displayed Him as a Man, a Glorified Man, at the center of a most glorious parade in the streets of Jerusalem. There are shouts of men and angels, trumpet blasts, whirling dancers, streamers, and thousands of flowers flowing through the air. It is all directed at one person: the Bridegroom. He is walking up to the temple on His coronation day, the Day when all Israel will be saved (Rom. 11:26). And the Father will crown Him with many crowns.

Jesus says yes to the Father's will. And He prays, *"Father, I desire that they also whom You gave Me may be with Me where I am, that they may behold My glory which You have given Me; for You loved Me before the foundation of the world"* (John 17:24).

JESUS DESIRES A BRIDE: practical assignment…answer the questions accordingly.

GROUP QUESTION: discuss whichever question seems most important.

1. Read Matt. 22:1-14; Mark 14:3-9; Rev. 19:1-10 (Especially Rev. 19:7).

2. From Rev. 19:7, write down what this verse shows about who God is.

3. From Rev. 19:7, write down what this verse shows about what God thinks and feels about you.

4. Do you believe that you are the bride of Christ?

5. Do you feel like the bride of Christ, loved by God, or a distant, forgotten person?

6. What, if anything, is keeping you from living today as the bride of Christ (meaning: what is keeping you from receiving His love today)?

7. Is there anything that you need to say sorry to God for (meaning: anything to ask His forgiveness for)? If so, write it in the space below. As you're writing it down, give Him all of your pain and regret.

8. If it is in the heart of the Father to bring the Bride together, in Christ, both Jew and Gentile (Isa. 49:6-7; Eph. 2:15; John 17:24), then what can you do to help this along?

9. **If you desire to live as the bride of Christ today, then pray this prayer:** "Jesus, I know that You are the Beloved Bridegroom. I know that You love the Father, and the Father loves Me the same way He loves You. I believe that You are _____ (summary of #2). I believe that you think and feel I am _____ (summary of #3). I know that I have the right to be loved by You. Fill me with Your overwhelming love, help me to live as the bride of Christ today."

ordinary people called to do extraordinary things

SIN HAPPENED….
Pre-Foundation #3

"**Therefore having these promises, beloved, let us cleanse ourselves from all filthiness of the flesh and spirit, perfecting holiness in the fear of God."** (2 Cor. 7:1)

GOAL
(**Step #1**) to understand and recognize sin attacking your life.
(**Step #2**) To overcome the effects of sin in your life.

When once asked, 'What is the definition of sin?' Billy Graham gave the following answer, "A sin is any thought or action that falls short of God's will. God is perfect, and anything we do that falls short of His perfection is sin. (1)" Everyone has sinned and fallen short of living perfect as God is perfect. Your sin is measurable before God and called "debt", or "the debt of sin"; and "the wages of sin is death" (Rom. 6:23). It is like an unpayable negative balance in your bank account. There are no earthly riches that can pay the debt of your sin. Only the most costly treasure of all, a perfect willing sacrifice (Jesus; John 1:29), can cover the debt of your sin. But where did sin come from?

God, before He created the Heavens and the earth, lived in perfect peace and harmony. But because He is PURE LOVE, He desired a family (that is you) to share His love with. Therefore, you were designed within the very heart of the Father, you were the very dream of His heart. However, satan, who was created by God, but chose to hate God and chose to hate you, constantly lies to people. He wants to deceptively convince you to turn away from God's commandments so that you will seek to do your own will, instead of God's Sovereign will. But this ultimately leads to your death and satan hideously laughing at your eternal demise. How does satan get you to sin? I am so glad you ask this. Truly this is the best question for you to ask.

Satan, who is an expert at lying and getting other people to believe lies, tries to influence your mind and actions. Then he wants to multiply your sinful actions, producing fruitlessness (the Father in Heaven wants you to be "fruitful", but satan is trying to kill you and use your "fruitlessness" to destroy others). How does he do this?

In the garden, God set up the perfect conditions for His children to love and serve Him, but satan unsuspectedly crept in to attack Adam and Eve. In the same way that satan deceived Adam and Eve, he now seeks to destroy humanity. Firstly, he (satan) wants to attack your mind by asking the question, "Did God really say?". He wants to get into your mind so you believe his lies (Adam and Eve believed the serpent; the consequence: they became sinners). Secondly, once you believe his lies, then satan provokes you to take actions that are against God's will—and this will destroy your life (Adam and Eve ate the fruit; the consequence: they were kicked out of the garden, and work became toilsome and painful; see Gen. 3:17-19). Thirdly, satan multiplies your sin against others, producing fruitlessness (Adam and Eve sinned; the consequence: one of their offspring killed the other; see Gen. 4:8). Sin's effects on humanity did not stop with Adam and Eve, for it was passed down to their children—and it has continued in this way to this very day. Sin is a sinister evil that still multiplies today.

Sin is multiplying. Satan is still working to attack people, day and night, because he hates us. Take, for instance, your life. He has tried to attack your mind; get you to believe lies so that you will constantly question, "Did God really say?". Then, after you believe the lie, he will try to provoke you to act accordingly. These sins may seem fun for a moment, but this feeling is always fleeting, and your momentary enjoyment will blow away like leaves on a windy day. Lastly, he will work to multiply this sin in your family and friends using you as the seed that goes into the ground and multiplies producing hurtful fruitlessness all around. BUT it does not have to end there.

Satan is simply out to multiply sin in our culture, using the same tactic over and over again. How? Firstly, through unrighteous movies, video games, and other forms of degrading media. Satan begins to ask the questions, "Did God really say?". For example, "Did God really say `all men are created in My image, in the image of God I created them both male and female`?" (Gen. 1:27). Secondly, once you believe satan's lie, he will get lots of people to follow through on their new found "progressive beliefs", with "forward thinking" actions. For example, if you believe God did not create men and women in the image of God, then you'll wrongly assume you can indulge in lustful actions against another, to discriminate against another race, and to choose who gets to be born or not. Lastly, your actions are then multiplied around you in fruitlessness. Following our example, your children's children will also devalue those around them in widespread war. Therefore, sin, which is a curse, is here to destroy you. But it does not have to end there with your destruction. *"For God so loved the world that He gave His only begotten son"* (John 3:16), Jesus (the Way, the Truth and the Life) that through the Cross of Christ...through the willing sacrifice...you might live.

How does sin affect culture? Let's discuss Thomas Jefferson, who took time to write the Declaration of Independence, which was an article that arguably inspired a nation and helped to shape many other nations to come. Also, Benjamin Franklin when helping to craft this document said, "With a firm reliance on the protection of Divine Providence". Further, John Adams, also helping with the original document added, "They are endowed by their

Creator with certain unalienable rights". Therefore, within that article was a phrase that is of particular interest. *"We hold these truths to be self-evident, that all men are created equal, that they are endowed by their Creator with certain unalienable Rights, that among these are Life, Liberty and the pursuit of Happiness. (2)"* Through these statements, we can determine that our Founding Fathers had a holy fear of the Lord and that they knew God made people for His good. However sin has crept across our land, attacking this very idea by saying, "Did God really say?" As a result, we see the rights of men, women and children in the womb devalued and trampled. Why? Because of the widespread advancement of sin. But sin will not be victorious because of the Father's Love displayed in the Cross.

ordinary people called to do extraordinary things

SIN HAPPENED: practical assignment…answer the questions accordingly.
GROUP QUESTION: discuss whichever question seems most important.

1. Do you agree with Billy Graham's definition of sin?

2. From the 1st paragraph (pg. 31; fill in the blank); your sin is measurable before God and called "debt", or "the debt of sin"; and "the wages of sin is _____" (Rom. 6:23)

3. From the 4th paragraph (pg. 32; fill in the blank): Firstly, he (satan) wants to attack your mind by asking the question, "_____?"

4. From the 4th paragraph (pg. 32; fill in the blank): "Secondly, once you believe satan's lies, then he gets you to take _____ against God, which will _____ your life".

5. From the 4th paragraph (pg. 32; fill in the blank): "Thirdly, satan _____ your sin against others, producing fruitlessness.

6. From the 6th paragraph (pg. 33; fill in the blanks): "Satan is simply out to _____ sin in our culture, using the same tactic, over and over again. How? Firstly, through unrighteous _____, video games, and other forms of degrading media. Satan begins to ask the questions, "Did God really say?".

7. According to the last sentence in this section, what is the Father's plan to defeat sin (pg. 34)?

8. On page #37 there is a "shape person", which represents you. Write on the shape all the sins that you have done, and all the sin that has been done to you. Just write them (in pen if you can). As the picture gets messier and messier, you will begin to see that this is satan's plan to mess up your life. Follow these directions:

Step 1: Write down your name.

Step 2: Make your picture personal, draw in your eyes, hair, nose (etc.).

Step 3: List (in the space provided) sin that you have done.

Step 4: List (in the space provided) sin that has been done to you.

Step 5: Draw on your picture your sin; everything you listed from (Steps 3 & 4)

9. **If you want freedom, then pray this prayer:** "Father I know that satan hates You and hates me. He is trying to attack my mind by getting me to say, "Did God really say?". And satan is trying to get me to sin: committing actions that are against your commandments, which will hurt myself and others. I acknowledge that this is wrong. I can see the picture of satan's plan to mess up my life. Help me to be set free from sin. Help me to forgive others and be forgiven. Show me the cross."

MY SIN

(Step 1) Write down your NAME:

(Step 2) Make your picture personal, draw in your eyes, hair, nose (etc.)

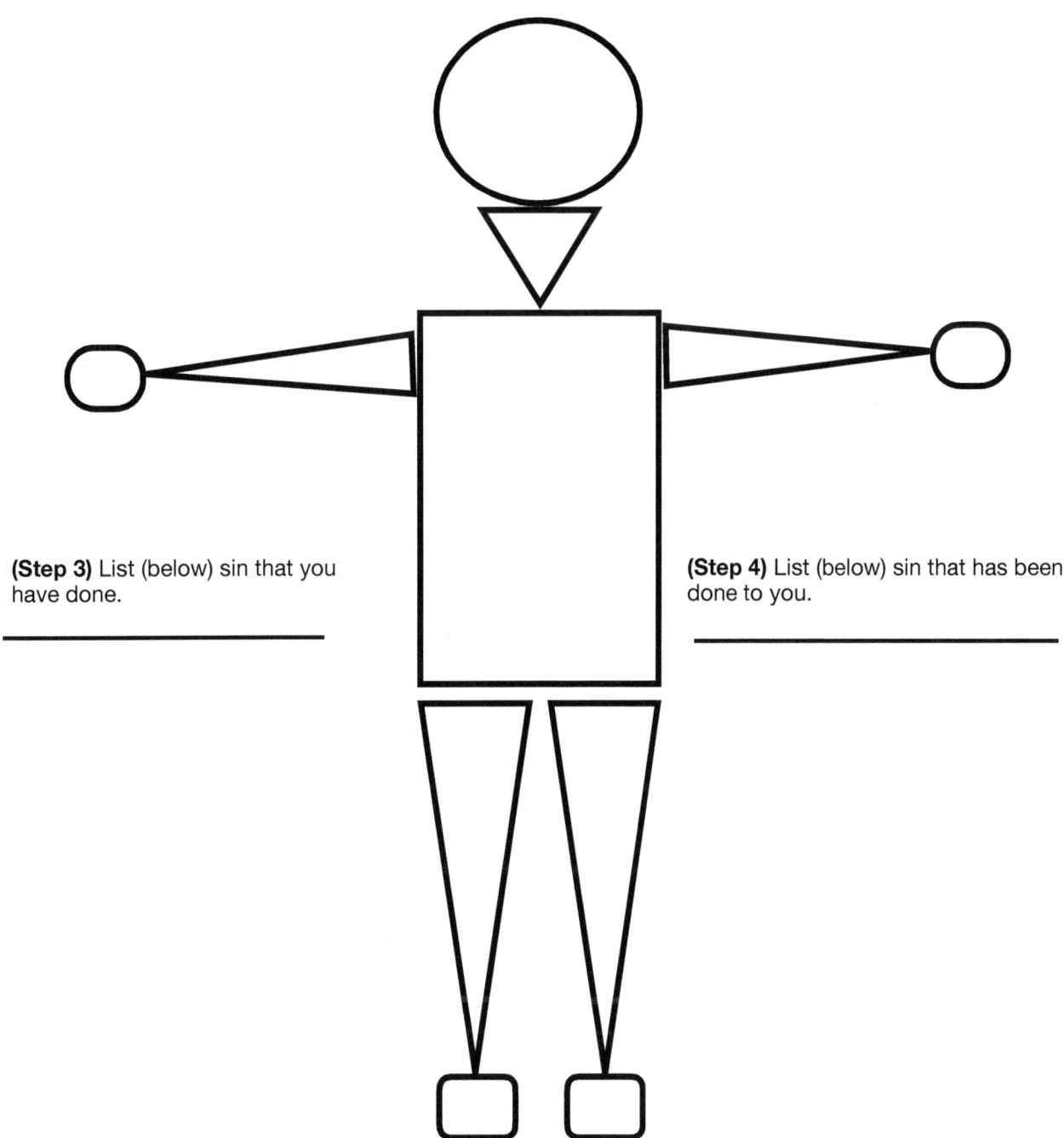

(Step 3) List (below) sin that you have done.

_____

(Step 4) List (below) sin that has been done to you.

_____

(Step 5) Draw on your picture your sin; everything you listed from (Step 3 & 4)

#happyholiness ©holyclubs.com

ordinary people called to do extraordinary things

THE CROSS....
Pre-Foundation #4

"...who Himself bore our sins in His own body on the tree (cross), that we, having died to our sins, might live for righteousness—by whose stripes you are healed." (1 Peter 2:24)

GOAL
(**Step #1**) To understand the life transforming power of the Cross.
(**Step #2**) Access the power of the Cross.

Do your sins make you feel distant from God? Does your sinful past haunt you daily? The cross of Christ has the power to restore you to worship God; to love Him and be loved by Him. The cross reveals the character of God: His love and justice. He loves the lost sinner, and His justice is perfect in your life. At the cross, those who turn to Him are delivered from the penalty of sin, the power of sin, and from the pain of sin. Truly, the cross is the place where the pain of sin is healed; the cross is more powerful than what has been done to you. If you suffer from ANY emotional problems—guilt, anxiety, depression, anger…etc.—there is healing in the cross of Christ (1 Peter 2:24; Heb. 12:2). If you are going through tragedy or suffering, there is absolute healing and peace as you meditate upon the cross: the Lamb that was slain for you. You receive God's righteousness and favor because of what Jesus did on the cross, not because of your good works (Rom. 3:21-31). To receive God's saving grace, it is necessary to sincerely repent.

For example, imagine a little girl growing up in a dysfunctional home. Her parents are separated, her brothers don't care, and her friends are equally as broken as she. On the outside she attempts to look like everything is ok, but inside her mind is racing with painful questions. Her shattered dreams have left her hopeless. Her once tender heart is bleeding from the shards of torn promises and empty love, while she hides behind a tattered wall of shame. She looks for love, searching desperately for something to grab hold of, only to have her now hardened heart, crushed over and over again. She needs a change.

Then one day she hears the inspirational, life-altering message of the cross. The Father loves her and wants her for His family, but her own sin (what she has done) is keeping her from Him. What's more the pain of what has been done to her is trying to keep her from reaching out to the love of God. But the loving truth of God knocks on the door of her heart, and she opens. She opens the door, just a little bit, but at least she opens the door. She prays a simple prayer, "Father, I repent, I was wrong, I chose my own way, please lead my life, please take this pain away, take my sin away." Instantly, Jesus—whose sacrifice on the cross paid for the debt of her sin, who gladly gave His life that she might live—He steps before the Father and intercedes so that all her wounds might be healed. Immediately, the Father in Heaven rejoices and explodes with lightning LOVE; all Heaven stops all their activities and rejoices with the Father. Why? Because what was lost has been found. The little girl, who was hopeless, now has hope in God. Jesus—the Way, the Truth, and the Life—makes her righteous. Immediately her eternal garments, which she will wear in Heaven, are automatically washed clean. She is justified before the Father in heaven; She is a New

Creation in Christ, and the Holy Spirit, her Counselor, who is God, will empower her, by grace, to be a New Creation in Christ.

THE CROSS AND FORGIVENESS

Whether you are the one sinned against (the victim), or the one who sinned against God and others (the aggressor), God has provided the way for you to forgive others and be forgiven, to receive mercy and walk forth in grace. But why is it important to enter into forgiveness?

Firstly, it is important that you are forgiven <u>from</u> your sin. Your forgiveness is based on a <u>historical</u> event—Jesus' death on the cross. A heavenly, holy, <u>legal</u> transaction occurred in God's court. Jesus paid the <u>debt</u> of your sin: that which was required to satisfy the demands of God's justice. Thus, Jesus' righteousness was credited to your account or imputed to you ([Rom. 4:6, 11, 23-24](#)). Everything that could disqualify you from receiving a new relationship with God was removed at the cross. When the Father looks upon you He sees you through the eyes of the finished work of the cross—bright shining and righteous and without spot or wrinkle.

Now you have to access God's bright and shining forgiveness by saying "yes" to Him and "no" to your old ways. This is how you start your own journey of holiness. This requires walking on God's path. When you turn away from God's path and "lean on your own understanding" (see [Prov. 3:5](#)), you are actively rejecting Jesus and following satan. In this is the essence of sin: to follow a path contrary to God's. All paths contrary to God's are of satan, and we have grown up being taught satan's paths (his ways). All satan's paths lead to death. But God, being rich in mercy, calls you to come back, to listen and learn from Jesus (His ways) so that you can walk in paths of righteousness. In this is the essence of repentance: to turn away from lies (satan's paths) and follow the truth (God's path). Our Father graciously gives you mercy instead of judgement. How? Because Jesus paid for the penalty of sin by dying on the cross, and when you are in Him, you are considered to have died with Him ([Rom. 6:8; Gal. 2:20](#)). If you died with Him, you will also live with Him, and so you do not have to fear the penalty of sin! Sin's power over you (death) is stripped away. In Christ, you have God's forgiveness, you are washed clean, your mind is renewed in the knowledge of the truth (Jesus and His path), and His grace empowers you to walk in paths of holiness before God. In this is the essence of holiness: to be forever in Christ — alive, clean, and continually walking in His path—conforming into His likeness—becoming holy as He is holy. This is God's amazing offer to you. He wants to give you a fresh start.

Next, it is important for you to forgive those that have sinned against you. You do this because God said to forgive others (He is Creator and we are the creation. Therefore we need to follow His Ways). Jesus taught us to pray for forgiveness and shared the consequences of not forgiving others. He said, "And forgive us our debts, As we forgive our debtors…*"For if you forgive men their trespasses, your heavenly Father will also forgive you. But if you do not forgive men their trespasses, neither will your Father forgive your trespasses"* (Matt. 6:12-15). It is what Jesus demonstrated on the cross. Even while dying a brutal and torturous death, He prayed, *"Father, forgive them! They do not know what they are doing."* (Luke 23:34) In this is the essence of forgiving others: choosing to let go of the pain and place justice in the hands of the good, good Father.

It is important to note that you are not giving up your Justice when you choose to forgive those who sinned against you. When you forgive someone, you give the pain to God and ask Him, the Just Fair Judge, to bring Heavenly Justice. This will be a merciful and just judgment; God desires that none would perish but all would come to repentance (2 Pt. 3:9). Asking for forgiveness and forgiving another allows God's love to grow in you (Luke 7:47), which thrusts you back in the race to "go" and make disciples of those around you (Matt. 28:19).

In conclusion, as Paul eloquently penned: *"Then comes the end, when He delivers the kingdom to God the Father, when He puts an end to all rule and all authority and power. For He must reign till He has put all enemies under His feet. The last enemy that will be destroyed is death. For `He has put all things under His feet.` But when He says `all things are put under Him,` it is evident that He who put all things under Him is excepted. Now when all things are made subject to Him, then the Son Himself will also be subject to Him who put all things under Him, that God may be all in all."* (1 Cor. 15:24-28).

THE CROSS: practical assignment…answer the questions accordingly.
GROUP QUESTION: discuss whichever question seems most important.

Giving your burdens to Jesus at the foot of the cross

1. Read (1 Peter 2:24; Heb. 12:2).

2. From (Heb. 12:2) What does this scripture tell you about who God is?

3. From (Heb. 12:2) What does this scripture tell you about what God thinks and feels about you?

4. From the 1st paragraph (pg. 39; fill in the blank): what are the three things the Cross has power to defeat:

    1) The _____ of sin.
    2) The _____ of sin.
    3) The _____ of sin.

5. Re-read (1 Peter 2:24). Do you believe that Jesus took the debt of your sin?

6. From the 5th paragraph (pg. 40; fill in the blank): "Firstly, it is important that you are forgiven _____ your sin. Your forgiveness is based on a _____ event—Jesus' death on the cross. A heavenly, holy, _____ transaction occurred in God's court. Jesus paid the _____ of your sin that was required to satisfy the claims of God's justice."

7. From paragraph #7 (pg. 41; fill in the blank): "Next, it is important for you to forgive those that _____ sinned against you. You do this because God _____ to forgive others (He is _____ and we are the creation. Therefore we need to follow His Ways)."

Now, in the space provided on page #45, give your sins to Jesus. How?

Step 1: Read Heb. 12:1 "Therefore we also, since we are surrounded by so great a cloud of witnesses, let us lay aside every weight (what has been done to you), and the sin (what you have done to others) which so easily ensnares us, and let us run with endurance the race that is set before us".

Step 2: Go to page #45 and personalize Jesus give Him: eyes, ears, noses, mouth, hair, and a crown of thorns.

Step 3: Go to page #45 and list your "weights" (sin that has been done to you).

Step 4: Go to page #45 and list your "sins" (what you are guilty of).

Step 5: One by one take your "weights" and your "sins" and GIVE them to Jesus. Write them across Jesus body. After you do this cross them off your list.

Step 6: Go to page #45. It is now time for you to officially nail your sin to the cross. Draw nails on the picture of Jesus's hands and feet. As you do remember, *"For God so loved the world, that He gave His only begotten Son"* (Jn. 3:16). God loves you. As you draw the nails give your sin to Him and He will set you free. You no longer have to carry this burden. Do this with a red pen if possible, write each one of your "weights and sins" (what you did, and what has been done to you) across the picture of Jesus (remember when you wrote them on the "sins page"? It is time to give them to Jesus). Write on His arms, His legs, His hands, and His face. Why? Because He loves you and wants to take your sins. (Note: take your time. When I first did this I wept with each sin). I realized two things:

REALIZATION #1: The sin done to me: Sin had caused me years of suffering. I was in pain. I was carrying things I did not need to carry. Also, you may have to forgive each person. Really forgive them. This means you are turning the whole situation over to God and allowing Him—the Perfect Just Judge—to handle the case for you. For example, as I recalled the bully in my life (the worst one), I cried thinking about what he did and then just said, "God I choose to forgive _____. I ask that you would set me free of this pain and please help him." Remember, if you forgive your brother God will also forgive you (Matt. 6:12).

REALIZATION #2: The sin that you did: I came to a realization that I had sinned. I could no longer take my sins lightly. My sin had nailed Jesus to the cross. With each sin that I wrote upon him I told Him I was sorry and asked Him to forgive me, and then I wept. It was a good cry.

9. **Lastly, after you have wept, write Jesus a "thank you" letter.**

Giving your burdens to Jesus at the foot of the Cross

(Step #1) Read Hebrews 12:1 "Therefore we also, since we are surrounded by so great a cloud of witnesses, let us lay aside every <u>weight</u> **(what has been done to you)**, and the <u>sin</u> **(what you have done to others)** which so easily ensnares us, and let us run with endurance the race that is set before us".

(Step #2) Personalize Jesus. Give Him: eyes, ears, noses, mouth, hair, and a crown of thorns.

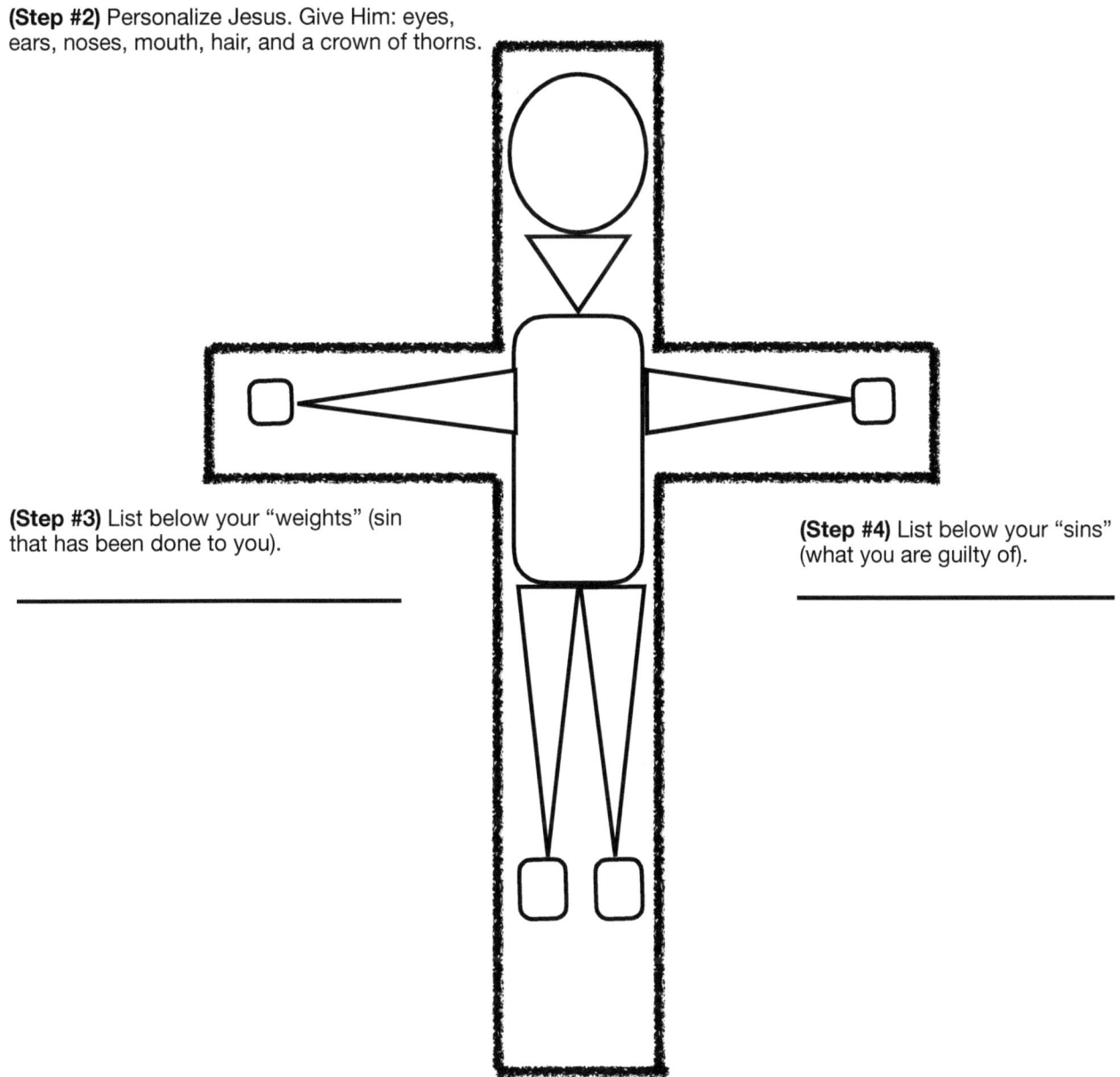

(Step #3) List below your "weights" (sin that has been done to you).

_____

(Step #4) List below your "sins" (what you are guilty of).

_____

(Step #5) One by one take your "weights" and your "sins" and **GIVE** them to Jesus. Write them across Jesus body (with a red pen). After you do this cross them off your list. You no longer have to carry them.

(Step #6) It is now time for you to officially nail your sins to the cross. Draw nails on the picture of Jesus's hands and feet.

#happyholiness ©holyclubs.com

ordinary people called to do extraordinary things

NEW CREATION
Pre-Foundation #5

Therefore, if anyone is in Christ, he is a new creation; old things have passed away; behold, all things have become new (2 Cor. 5:17)

GOAL
(Step #1) To understand and believe the (2 Cor. 5:17)
(Step #2) To walk in freedom, as a "New Creation" in Christ!

Every person has struggled with sin, missed the mark, and has a few chapters of their life story that they may want to erase. But there is good news! The story does not have to end there. Jesus, the uncreated Author and Finisher of your Faith, the One who is loved by the Father and loves you that same way ([John 15:9](#)), died on the Cross to Redeem you—restoring you to the Father. He made you a "new creation", if you are in Christ ([2 Corin. 5:17](#)). Why? Because He has the desire (God first loved us; [John 3:16](#)) and power (the Word and Spirit) to make you a new creation in Christ.

Imagine a little child, abandoned, hungry, sleeping in the cold streets, and fending for her life continually. Then one day, she wakes up to a commotion around her. The President of the United States, with a large fleet of secret service agents, comes to this child's makeshift shelter of boxes. The President approaches the child, picks her up, and places her into his car. He says, "today is the best day of your life. I am giving you 100 billion dollars. All you have to do is take this check down to the bank and cash it." In a moment, she is a new creation.

But her struggle does not end there. She still has to access the money. Until she goes to the bank and cashes the check, she is just a 12 year old with the chance to be a billionaire.

This girl has spent 12 years of her life living on the streets, so she acts like a person from the streets. She will have to change on the inside so that that she can live like a billionaire. She will go from sleeping on the streets to the best of homes. She will move from eating out of the trash to eating in the finest restaurants. She will go from living with friends from the streets to interacting with friends of wealth. She must go to the bank and become a new creation so that she can enjoy the benefits of a billionaire.

So how does she access the 100 billion dollars? Or more importantly, how do you become a new creation? You must turn from your sins and call out to Jesus, the Redeemer—then you are restored to God the Father in Christ the Son. All who are in Christ receive a new position, new power, new desires, new insights and new destiny in God—the free gift of God—righteousness in Christ.

Simplifying the free gift of righteousness.

I summarize God's righteousness in three stages:

    A. **Justification**: your <u>legal</u> position—past tense, focused on my spirit

       (I have been saved).

    B. **Sanctification:** your <u>living</u> condition—present tense, focused on your soul

       (I am being saved).

    C. **Glorification:** your <u>eternal</u> exaltation—future tense, focused on your body

       (I will be saved).

Instantly at your new birth, you are justified ("just-as-if-you-never-sinned"), receiving God's righteousness freely and fully (100%). This happens when you ask Jesus to be Lord over your life. You are being sanctified as God's resurrection power (see below) conforms you to God's Word and the Holy Spirit. His GRACE takes you further on the journey to be holy just as God the Father is holy. You will be glorified as you rule and reign with God forever.

(NOTE) Resurrection Power: The Father raised Christ from the dead. This same power will raise you from the dead; in Christ, you are a new creation that walks holy in the grace of God. Your water baptism is union with Christ. When you go under water, your sins are dead and you come up "sin-free" and alive. Paul says, *"For if we have been united together in the likeness of His death, certainly we also shall be in the likeness of His resurrection"* (Rom. 6:5). When Jesus came out of the baptismal water, He was made alive; so you are made alive at your baptism. The Father raised Jesus from the dead—Resurrection Power. In the same way, when you are baptized, He imparts "new (newness of) life" to believers. Day-by-day, we walk in a "newness (a new kind) of life". This shows outwardly that the believer has received new life (2 Cor. 5:17). The same power that raised Christ from the dead is here for you to walk holy today. God's resurrection power in you will help you overcome sin and sickness.

Your standing with God (as a new creation) is not based on what you do. Instead, it is based on what Jesus did, and how you are able to cooperate with God's plan. God did His part. And you must do yours. What is His part? He died on the cross to take away the debt of your sin, and He gives us His resurrection power to walk in the newness of life. What is your part? An excellent question, and one that could change the very course of your life. You must cooperate with GRACE. How much you cooperate with the grace of God, in the ways that Scripture teaches, will determine how holy you become (this is the process of "being sanctified").

As you receive the free gift of righteousness, you will be affected in three areas: (1) legal, (2) emotional, and (3) spiritually. Firstly, you receive a new legal position with the free gift of righteousness (remember: you are justified). As a child of God, you stand in the Father's presence with confidence that you are fully accepted, enjoyed and loved. He is not secretly thinking about what you once did, nor is He thinking about your future shortcomings. No! Jesus made a way for you to live righteously before God the Father. How is this possible? Your new position is based on a historical event—Jesus' death on the cross. A heavenly, holy, legal transaction occurred in God's court. Jesus paid the debt of your sin that was required to satisfy the claims of God's justice (God's wrath is poured out on sin; the debt of your sin leads to death). Thus, Jesus' righteousness was credited to your account or imputed to you (Rom. 4:6, 11, 23-24). Everything (and I mean every little thing) that could disqualify you from receiving a new relationship with God was removed at the cross. When the Father looks upon you He sees you through the eyes of the finished work of the cross—bright shining and righteous, without spot or wrinkle.

Secondly, God redeems your <u>emotional</u> position with His free gift of righteousness. All who receive the gift of righteousness are freely <u>enjoyed</u> and <u>delighted</u> in by God from the moment you are born again. Right away, despite what you have done, you can begin to feel His affection for you. The Cross of Christ opens wide the door for you to love God, and to receive His Love. Once you were miles away from God, but now you are face-to-face. The Kindest Man Alive—King Jesus—delights in you!

Lastly, the free gift of righteousness renews your spiritual position. You have a new nature. The <u>old</u> is gone and the <u>new</u> is here. In a moment, you are transferred from satan's kingdom, where he viciously hates you, and you are cradled, like a newborn baby, in the Father's <u>strong</u> and <u>protective</u> arms. Your spirit is made righteous and indwelt by the Spirit of God (2 Cor. 5:21; Eph. 4:24; Col. 3:10). You should encourage your friends on a near daily basis, reminding them that they are new creations in Christ Jesus (if, in fact, they are in Christ). Remember, you are responsible for each other: to grow in the first commandment, and to enter into the fullness of God's destiny for each other. You are called to be your brother and sister's keeper.

Ok, if I am a "new creation", then why do I still feel bad and have the urge to sin? Now, when you are righteous before God, you no longer live under the reign of sin. During the reign of sin, you were held in condemnation (judgment) before God, and you were powerless before sin (at the heart level), sickness, and satanic attacks. You had no ability within your strength to change things. You had no power to resist the sinful temptations in your heart (fear, anger, pride, anxiety, bitterness, lust, envy, etc.). You were in darkness without the ability to understand God and His Word or to receive divine direction for your life. Also, you were destitute and without a lasting purpose or vision of hope and a future in God. Now as a new creation in Christ, no longer under the reign of sin, you are free from the power of sin. However, you may still feel to urge to sin, because your old man (old patterns of thought) still try to control your will. Each one of these "old patterns" must come under the will of God. This is where you are being sanctified. Remember, you're justified before God in heaven, but you're being sanctified, and you will be glorified.

What changes when you are a NEW CREATION, ALIVE IN GOD? In the reign of grace, you instantly receive a new position (before God in Heaven), new power (to use the Name of Jesus), new desires (love God and be loved by Him, while loving your neighbor), and new insights (divine revelation of God's word). Remember, you just have to access the 100 billion dollar check. This position is referred to as being "alive to God" ([Rom. 6:11, 13; Eph. 2:1, 5; Col. 2:13; 1 Pet. 3:18](#)). Immediately, you have God's divine acceptance with tender affection. He enjoys and delights in relating to you as a child of God and the Bride of Christ. There is no condemnation or rejection from God ([Rom. 8:1](#)).

In the reign of grace, you have the power of the Holy Spirit, which gives you new power with new desires and insights so that you may know God, His Word, and His will. You received supernatural power to resist sin and satan. You received a new nature when your spirit was born again and made righteous. Also, in the reign of grace, you were given the authority to speak the name of Jesus to release the works of God and destroy the works of Satan in your life and circumstances, as well as in others'.

In the reign of grace, you are able to have hope and see your divine destiny. You have a good future in God as one who will forever reign with Him. Everyday is relevant! What you do today affects your eternal life before Him—for He gives you eternal rewards for your faithfulness, even faithfulness in the small things (Lk. 19:17).

Remember: our 12 year old (in the above story) has to leave the reign of sin and turn to the reign of grace. She has to approach the bank with the 100 billion dollar check in hand and tell them "who she is". Imagine if a homeless girl went to the bank and said, "Give me 100 billion dollars". She would be laughed out of the bank! But what if the president went with her? What if they both stood in the bank and he said, "I endorse this check. She has a new position, new power, new desires, and new insights." The bank would then allow her to have the funds. In the same way, Jesus, at the cross, justified you by taking your sin away so that you no longer live in the reign of sin—He empowered you to enter into the reign of grace.

In summary, understanding who we are as a new creation "in Christ" involves the following truths.

1. First, you have a new Heavenly legal position that you received in Christ, which is the gift of righteousness and the indwelling Spirit. You are bright and shiny before God in Heaven. The old is gone. The new is here.

2. Next, your earthly daily living condition is renewed as you believe. This is a lifestyle of righteousness. Day-by-day, your countenance, your heart, your thoughts, your eyes, your hands, your work ethic, what you watch, what you listen to, what you think in your mind, how you interact with family and coworkers—this all changes for the best.

3. Also, you are revived in your affectionate relationship as God's beloved, standing as the Father's child and Jesus' Bride. Your heart will grow in love with God.

4. Lastly, you grow in anointed partnership as you are a coworker with Jesus, using your authority in Christ to "GO" and make disciples, and building up the church into the head, which is Christ (Col. 1:18).

In Conclusion: the Process of Grace.

Therefore, you must understand the process of GRACE and believe in His words, while following the Holy Spirit. This means you are at war! Yes, even you. This is true because the one lying to you—that deceiver, "LIE"CIFER—hates you and wants to destroy you. He is at war with you, and God is at war with him. Also, you are at war with your sinful flesh, evil thoughts, and the corrupted day-to-day earthly living conditions, all which try to draw your mind and actions away from God. Today, believe the words of Paul and believe that the resurrection power of God is stronger than the sin that binds you and the recurring thoughts that attack you. *"As sin reigned in death, even so grace might reign through… Jesus…. How shall we who died to sin [permanently freed from the reign of sin] live any longer in it?"* (Rom. 5:21-6:2). God's power over sin is greater than your ability to bring freedom to yourself.

NEW CREATION: practical assignment…answer the questions accordingly.
GROUP QUESTION: discuss whichever question seems most important.

1. Read (2 Cor. 5:17). What does the Scripture tell you about who God is? What does this Scripture tell you about what God thinks and feels about you?

2. Fill in the blanks (pg. 48) with the texts above: "Simplifying the free gift of righteousness. I summarize God's righteousness in three stages:

    A. **Justification:** your _____ position—past tense, focused on my spirit
       (I have been saved)

    B. **Sanctification:** your _____ condition—present tense, focused on your soul
       (I am being saved)

    C. **Glorification:** your _____ exaltation—future tense, focused on your body
       (I will be saved)"

3. In paragraph 10 (pg.49; fill in the blanks): "Firstly, you receive a new legal position with the free gift of righteousness (remember, you are justified). As a _____, you stand in the Father's presence with _____ that you are fully accepted, _____ and loved."

4. In paragraph 11 (pg. 50; fill in the blanks): "Secondly, God redeems your _____ position with His free gift of righteousness. All who receive the gift of righteousness are freely _____ and _____ in by God from the

moment you are born again."

5. In paragraph 12 (pg. 50; fill in the blanks): "Lastly, the free gift of righteousness renews your spiritual position. You have a new nature. The _____ is gone and the _____ is here. In a moment, you are transferred from satan's kingdom, where he viciously hates you, and you are cradled, like a newborn baby, into the Father's _____ and _____ arms."

6. **Instructions for (page 57)** "New Creation" (NAME): In the space provided on (page 57), you will give yourself a new name (Rev. 2:17). This does not mean you have to call yourself by the new name. However God will give you a new name. Many people have "new names", which you find on social media. So take time to write in the new name. For example, I just called myself "Benjamin" because the old guy "Ben" was the one that did all the sinning. And "Benjamin" means "beloved son of My Right Hand".

7. **Further, instructions for (page 57)** "New Creation" (BODY/SPIRIT/MIND): In the drawing of your "new creation" (page 57), you will take each area of your body and write in "new" and then the body part (write on the drawing, so that you know God is making you new; the old is gone and the new has come). As you do, ask God to redeem that area. For example, on your mind, write, "I have a new mind" and pray, "the old mind is gone, and in Christ I have a new mind—therefore redeem me and make me new." Fill in all these areas (and write in any others). Take your time and believe in His desire to make you a new creation and not your passion to make yourself new. Turn the page marked "New Creation" and follow these steps:

Step 1: Write down your NAME:

Step 2: Make your picture personal, draw in your eyes, hair, nose (etc.).

Step 3: God will redeem your sins; look at your sin(s) from the "My Sins" sheet (page 37); instead of sin write the redemption of your sin (ex. anger - patience; lust - purity; envy - generous; pride - meekness).

Step 4: You are now a new creation; write down the "Fruit of the Spirit" on your picture: love, joy, peace, long-suffering, kindness, goodness, faithfulness, gentleness, self-control (Galatians 5:22-23).

Step 5: You are now a New Creation; write down the "NEW" aspects of your life on your picture: New mind, New heart, New hands, New lips, New eyes, New body, New desires, New revelation, New passions, New strength, Etc. (keep going).

Step 6: Jesus taught the "Sermon on the Mount" as the constitution for your life as a New Creation; write this list on the picture of the new you: Blessed are the poor in spirit (humble); Blessed are those that mourn; Blessed are the meek; Blessed are those who hunger and thirst for righteousness; Blessed are the merciful; Blessed are the pure in heart; Blessed are the peacemakers; Blessed are those who are persecuted for righteousness' sake (Matt. 5:1-11).

NEW CREATION

(Step 1) Write down your NAME:

(Step 2) Make your picture personal, draw in your eyes, hair, nose (etc.).

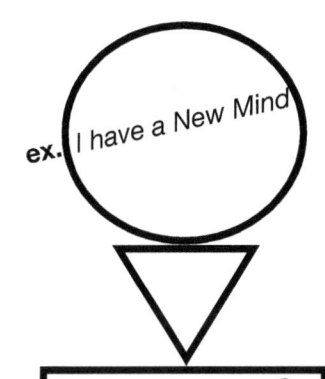

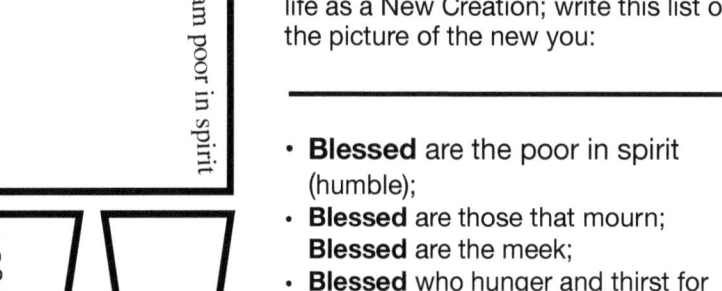

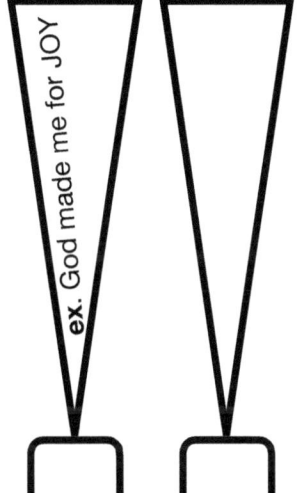

(Step 3) God will redeem your sins; look at your sin(s) from the "My Sins" sheet; instead of your sin(s) write the redemption of your sin (ex. anger - patience; lust - purity; envy - generous; pride - meekness).

(Step 4) You are now a new creation; write down the fruit of the Spirit.

- love
- joy
- peace
- long-suffering
- kindness
- goodness
- faithfulness
- gentleness
- self-control

(Step 5) You are now a new creation; write down the "NEW" aspects of your life on your picture. (be creative)

- New Mind
- New Heart
- New Hands
- New Lips/Words
- New Eyes
- New Body
- New Desires
- New Revelation
- New Passions
- New Strengths

(Step 6) Jesus taught the Sermon on the Mount as our constitution for your life as a New Creation; write this list on the picture of the new you:

- **Blessed** are the poor in spirit (humble);
- **Blessed** are those that mourn; **Blessed** are the meek;
- **Blessed** who hunger and thirst for righteousness;
- **Blessed** *are* the merciful; **Blessed** *are* the pure in heart;
- **Blessed** *are* the peacemakers;
- **Blessed** *are* those who are persecuted for righteousness' sake

#happyholiness   ©holyclubs.com

ordinary people called to do extraordinary things

OVERCOMING TEMPTATIONS
Pre-Foundation #6

"No temptation has overtaken you except such as is common to man; but God is faithful, who will not allow you to be tempted beyond what you are able, but with the temptation will also make the way of escape, that you may be able to bear it." (1 Corinthians 10:13)

GOAL:

- **(Step 1)** To be aware of temptation.
- **(Step 2)** To overcome temptation.

A temptation is the evil **desire** to do something that is foolish and unwise, which will result in harm to you and others (remember, satan tempted Eve by saying, *"did God really say"*; [Gen. 3:1).](#) **Inward sin** is birthed when you willingly "think about", or envision, how the particular temptation will benefit you (remember, Eve thought about how eating the fruit would be beneficial to her; [Gen. 3:6](#)). **Outward sin** happens when you willingly act upon the tragic temptation (Adam and Eve ate the fruit; [Gen. 3:6](#)). **Pain** is what results after you sin (Adam and Eve were ashamed of their full nakedness; [Gen. 3:7](#)).

Satan is a deceitful tempter. He hates God and viciously wants to destroy you. His single purpose is to destroy the dream on the Father's heart, which is you, and keep you from being loved as a child of God in the Father's family. He also wants to keep you from walking as the Bride of Christ and being loved by Jesus—the Beloved Bridegroom, Glorious King and Just Judge. He wants to tempt you to disobey God and build your own kingdom. The Bible says he is *"like a roaring lion, seeking whom he may devour"* ([1 Peter 5:8](#)). Have you seen those nature documentaries? I am talking about the frightening ones, that initially show a large, peaceful herd of pleasantly grazing animals. A ravenous lion crouches in the bushes nearby, just waiting to tear apart some unsuspecting straggler. Usually, the lion isn't alone. It approaches the herd, working together as an evil pack, separating the weak or young, and devouring them. In the same way, satan and his tormenting minions try to creep their way into your life, tempting you by filling your head with lies, and pulling you away from the herd (the church). This leads only to ruin. Satan is always trying to brutally tempt you away from God to your destruction.

He shrewdly tempted Adam and Eve in the garden; he got them to doubt by asking, "did God really say?" He tempted David, the warrior king. After a long battle to obtain God's promises for himself and Israel, he ends up falling into adultery and murder—and he suffers the consequences until the last days of his kingdom ([2 Sam. 12:9-15](#)). Satan also tempted Jesus for 40 days in the wilderness, and only departed to seek a more opportune time ([Matt. 4:1-3](#)). But Jesus overcame the temptation of satan. He never sinned. He is the perfect, sinless man. Then, with His death on the cross, He made a way for you also to overcome temptation. But what will you do when satan tempts you?

The book of Revelation declares that satan will accuse you before the Father in Heaven. It kind of goes like this.

God: (He talks first, because satan can't even blink without God allowing him.) "Satan, what are you doing today?"

Satan: "Well, as you know, Ben fell into temptation. Therefore, I want to mess up his life. I am going to start by trying to disqualify him in three ways: First, I will try to convince him that You (God) are mad at him for sinning and then I will tell him that his future is a failure. Second, I will try to convince him that other people don't like him because of his sin. Third, I will try to convince him his identity is not what You intended it to be; I'll tell him he is a sinner, not a son."

The conversation may go something like that. But that is not the end. Do you know what is next? (This is the question you should ask, if you are really seeking wisdom.) However, if you like pain and are not searching for wisdom, then you can put the book down and just go on your way...BUT, if you desire a change, then read on…

Once satan has accused you before the Father, he will then shrewdly and deceivingly work to disqualify you. He does this by deliberately making you to feel like you are not worthy to follow Christ. How does He do this? He attacks you by filling your mind with negative lie after lie. Then his last, but certainly not least, cruel tactic will be to tempt you to sin further. He says, "well since you've already sinned, why not just do it again?" Then he can start the whole evil process over again, drowning you in the cycle of pain, woe, and regret. Thankfully, it does not have to end there because God, the good Father, made a way to stop the cycle of gut wrenching despair. Let me teach you to overcome. That's right—I am NOT gonna do it for you. Instead, I will show you the path to rise up in the strength of Christ and overcome.

How do you overcome? You overcome, *"by the blood of the Lamb and by the word of their testimony, and they did not love their lives to the death"* (Rev. 12:11). Adam and Eve, after they were kicked out of the garden, could not overcome in their own strength. Jesus, the Living Word, came in the cool of the day, covered them, and set them back into a place where they were graciously redeemed. David, though he struggled because of sin, ran to the

Mercy of God, repented, and was made new (Ps. 51:11). In the end, it was said about his life that he was a man after God's own heart, and he did the will of God in his life (Acts 13:22; 1 Samuel 13:14). Also, David still has promises of God in the Millennial Kingdom (Ezekiel 37:25). And Jesus ultimately overcame temptation by quoting the word of God, and so should you (Lu. 4:1-13).

Maybe, you feel a little bit like David felt after he committed his sins. Remember, he got Bathsheba pregnant, killed her husband Uriah to try and cover things up, and then had to deal with major family issues (2 Sam. 12:9-15). But he returned to the Lord. He returned to the Mercy of the Lord (God's Mercy is that He does NOT give you what you deserve); David, repented and God washed Him clean. Yes, he still suffered consequences, but God restored him. I want to tell you plainly: no matter how disqualified you feel, God can and wants to restore you. Turn to Him. Repent, ask Him for mercy, and let God skillfully write the next season of your life. David had his greatest days ahead of him—and so can you. Paul says, as one star differs from another, so will you in the age to come (1 Corinthians 15:40-42). In other words, the deeper you pursue your individual path of holiness, the greater this will reflect in your heavenly garment in the age to come. So, even if you feel disqualified, get back into the game, just like David. The best is yet to come! (I always looks at my life on earth like an internship. It actually counts, but what I do now positions myself to serve God in the age to come).

Have you ever considered the ant and the grasshopper? An ant works with others to build a home and to gather food for the winter. However, the grasshopper does neither: when the cold comes, it falls and dies. Which are you?

I want to be the ant. I want to build with others, gather food, and live safe and snug in the winter. I want to overcome when the cold comes. It is the same for you and me. The cold time is coming (the time of temptation). Don't be like the unsuspecting grasshopper. Instead, quickly prepare using these simple techniques.

TEMPTATION: practical assignment…answer the questions accordingly.
GROUP QUESTION: discuss whichever question seems most important.

1. **First**: Remember, they overcame by the Blood of the Lamb and the word of their testimony; you must accept Christ into your life. When you do, the Blood of God will take away the debt of your sin, reconcile you to worship Him, and then thrust you into a holy lifestyle. **Task**: if you are not saved, then watch this video now (My Hope America).

2. **Second:** Know that temptation will come. Affirm in your heart that you don't want to sin. **Task**: write a note to God, asking Him to lead you not into temptation and to deliver you from evil (Matt. 6:8-13).

3. **Third**: Jesus overcame by quoting the Word of God. So read your Bible daily and believe what it says. Conform to the word of God; don't try to conform the word to your lifestyle. **Task**: commit to reading your bible 5 days a week. Put it in your planner.

4. **Fourth**: Allow the power of the Holy Spirit to transform you. The Holy Spirit is there to comfort, to lead, to teach and to empower you to walk holy. **Task**: Prayerfully ask the Holy Spirit to lead you not into temptation and to deliver you from evil (Matt. 6:8-13).

5. **Fifth**: Seek to live holy. God is holy and He desires the best for you; namely, for you to go on the journey of being holy like Him. **Task**: pray and ask God to take you on a journey to be holy like Him (1 Peter 1:16).

6. **Lastly**: Get connected to the local church. **Task**: find a church that preaches Jesus.

7. **Wait**…this should be the last task: Seek to walk in humility and to be empowered by His Grace. **Task**: turn the page and begin your journey of humility.

ordinary people called to do extraordinary things

HUMILITY
Pre-Foundation #7

"And being found in appearance as a man, He humbled Himself and became obedient to the point of death, even the death of the cross. Therefore God also has highly exalted Him and given Him the name which is above every name." (Philippians 2:8-9)

GOAL:

(**Step#1**) To understand God's humility.

(**Step #2**) To become clothed in humility day and night.

Goal: to understand God's humility and become clothed in humility day and night.

Humility: submission and utter dependence upon God; belief and trust in God's Word and Holy Spirit. Also, understanding and desire to be clothed in humility on a daily basis.

Pride: exalting yourself in thoughts or deed above God and or other people; thinking of yourself more highly than you ought ([Rom. 12:4](#)); assuming it is alright for you to ignore God and then choosing to sin ([Dan. 4:28-33](#)).

God is Holy: God said *"be holy as I am holy"* ([1 Peter 1:16](#)). Also, God is humble and calls you to take His yoke of humility upon yourself ([Matt. 11:29](#)). Jesus, who is God, perfectly displayed the humility of God by leaving heaven, lowering Himself to become a human, dying upon the cross so that you might live, and then giving Himself to intercession unto the Father's will being accomplished.

Satan: who hates God and hates you, was created by God to be a worship leader, but he exalted himself (became prideful) above God ([Ezekiel 28:11-19](#)). He then lead a rebellion of fallen angels against God, and slipped into the Garden of Eden where he knowingly released the poison of pride into the minds and hearts of Adam and Eve. Today, he seeks to get all to of humanity to walk in pride, live in idolatry, and turn away from worshipping God.

Garden of Eden: The perfect place for God to raise a family; a place where you can choose to live free, love God and love each other. After meditating upon the ways of satan, Adam and Eve choose to eat the fruit of pride, and sin grew in their hearts. As a result, they were humiliated and had to leave the Garden of Eden, toil with the land, and eventually perish. But, it does not have to end in death.

Heaven: The Father desires an eternal family to cherish and to love, and Jesus is looking for a Bride. Even though sin and pride caused you to die, God (who desires that none would perish and who loves you with an Everlasting Love; 2 Peter 3:9) made a way for you to be set free from the wages of sin and death. He made a way for you to be alive in Heaven evermore by sending His Son, Jesus, to pay the debt of your sin, washing away the guilt and shame of your sin, empowering you by His Grace to walk alive in the Holy Spirit, while partnering with you in bringing many others into His Saving Grace.

What is the path of humility?

1. **Pride:** If you are in rebellion against God, then you must humble yourselves (submit to God's Word and Spirit), and Repent: turn to God AND change your ways to become His ways.

2. **Humiliation:** If you do not humble yourselves before God, then you will be humiliated (ashamed as fools) by God, because God resists the proud, but gives Grace to the humble (James 4:6). God does this because He loves you and has great plans for your life; He wants you to turn from your ways and live holy before Him (John 3:16).

3. **Clothed in humility:** Daily, you must humble yourselves before the Word of God and the Holy Spirit. Ask God every day to show you the areas of your life that He wants to change. Through day-by-day prayer and meditation, you conform to the image of God. You do this with God's gracious help, by allowing God to confront sin in your life, and becoming the person He is asking you to be. There are so many rewards when you do this! Rewards both now and in the age to come (Lu. 14:11).

What does it look like to DAILY clothe yourself in Humility?

1. **Jesus:** He is God and He is humble; Jesus is lowly and humble in heart. He came to earth as a human. Paul preaches. *"Let this mind be in you which was also in Christ Jesus, who, being in the form of God, did not consider it robbery to be equal with God, but made Himself of no reputation, taking the form of a bondservant, and*

coming in the likeness of men ([Philippians 2:5-7](#))". Jesus was clothed in humility; He lowered Himself to become a man; He humbled Himself to only do and say the Father's will ([John 5:19](#)); He humbled Himself and became involved in the daily struggles and squabbles of the 12 disciples as He diligently served them in discipleship ([Mark 8:13-21](#)). He humbled Himself and washed the disciples feet. He humbled Himself to the place of being physically beaten and died disgracefully upon the cross. Also, He humbled Himself to being a man (with a glorified body) in Heaven forever ([Dan. 7:13-14](#)).

2. **Word of God and the Holy Spirit:** God's Word and Spirit are Holy, Perfect, and Righteous altogether. You are prideful when you assume that you are above God's Word and the leading of the Holy Spirit (such as Herod, who exalted himself above God and found himself attacked by worms and dying; [Acts 12:1-4](#)). However, <u>you are clothed in humility</u> when you search the scriptures, live in community (the body of Christ), while conforming to the Word of God and leading of the Holy Spirit.

3. **Sin:** Sin is the opposite of what God deems as righteous. You are prideful when you feel that you can whimsically do whatever you want instead of following God's ways. <u>You are clothed in humility</u> when you follow God's ways. Also, your past sin keeps you humble; it is not sin, but God's transforming grace at work in your life, which constantly reminds you of who you used to be. Therefore, it is His Mercy and Grace, which are at work in your life, that keeps you humble.

4. **Sin (part 2):** May God enlighten your eyes, because your thoughts, words, and feelings towards those around you are a test of your humility towards Him. You are prideful when you think of yourself as above the sin of another person. <u>You are clothed in humility</u> when you allow God to show you His love for those around you (even those that have hurt you) ([Rom. 12:3](#)). Also, know that it is only because of the

grace of God that you are not struggling with the sins you see in them.

5. **Chastening:** Everyone wants to be a son or daughter of God, but not everyone wants to endure the chastening of the Lord. The writer of Hebrews states, *"And you have forgotten the exhortation which speaks to you as to sons: `My son, do not despise the chastening of the Lord, Nor be discouraged when you are rebuked by Him; For whom the Lord loves He chastens, And scourges every son whom He receives. If you endure chastening, God deals with you as with sons; for what son is there whom a father does not chasten? But if you are without chastening, of which all have become partakers, then you are illegitimate and not sons`"* (Heb. 12:5-7). You are prideful if you think yourself above God's righteous (yet loving) hand of discipline. <u>You are clothed in humility</u> when you allow God's Word and Spirit to become the #brand: the "pages" you "scroll through", "like", "comment-on" and conform to day-by-day.

6. **Finances:** Historically, most people do not have enough finances. This is either because we spend more than we make, or we do not have the means to create the necessary wealth for daily living. Either way, this is very humbling. Jesus said, *"it is harder for a rich man to enter into heaven then for a camel to go through the eye of a needle"* (the "eye of the needle" in the original text is actually a small opening in the wall of an ancient city; Matt. 19:23-24). Furthermore, Jesus calls you to forsake the world's ways and diligently walk the "narrow path" of the Lord's Righteousness (Matt. 7:13-14). You must "take off" the things that are hindering you from following God along His narrow path. Two bulky strongholds weighing you down (in the area of finances) are greed and fear. You are prideful when you keep your funds for your kingdom. You are fearful when you believe that God, who provides for the birds of the air (Matt. 6:26), will not provide for you. Therefore, <u>you are clothed in humility</u> before God when you trust your Heavenly Father and give to Him your tithes and offerings. This allows God, who sees in secret, to exalt (lavishly

reward) you in His time (Matt. 6:1-4).

7. **Prayer:** God's design is for prayer to be the means by which you stay humble. God has the plan for His Kingdom Come. He releases the plan through His Word and by the Holy Spirit. Together, believers wait upon and pray until He answers from on High. And when the nation is in a season of judgment, God calls you to humble yourselves with other believers in prayer (2 Chron. 7:14). You are prideful when you assume that you don't have to pray. You are clothed in Humility when you seek His face, turn from your ways, pray to your Father who is in secret, and wait upon Him to answer (instead of going out to make something happen).

8. **Testimonies:** Giving a testimony about what God has done in your life (in a proper way, of course) can be a very powerful tool. However, sharing a testimony and glorifying yourself will hurt you and the body of Christ. You are prideful when your actions are the center of the story, or you promote yourself instead of the Kingdom of God. You are clothed in Humility when you first share the testimony in private to God and then share it with others—that is, if He asks you. This will promote God and bring all glory to Him. Glorifying yourself by giving a testimony is a very serious issue that must be confronted. For example, you are clothed in humility when you say, "I prayed for the person and they were healed in Jesus Name." Instead of, "I healed this person of their disease and know my ministry is going viral." Yes, your ministry has a virus, but God willing it will not go viral. Humility attracts heaven, while putrid pride promotes hell.

9. **Discipling others:** Jesus served, and He has called you to serve the body of Christ with your talents. Jesus taught, *"For who is greater, he who sits at the table, or he who serves? Is it not he who sits at the table? Yet I am among you as the One who serves"* (Luke 22:27). You are clothed in humility when you choose to love and serve those who are mean, hurtful, immature, and sinful. Remember, Jesus served

the disciples into their calling and so should you (mom's and dad's, your number one "small group" is your spouses and family; they are your highest priority).

10. **Being Discipled:** It is important that all of us are humble and submitted to discipleship from safe, Godly leadership (i.e. church, ministry, small group family type setting, etc.). Jesus said to His disciples, *"If anyone desires to come after Me, let him deny himself, and take up his cross, and follow Me."* (Matt. 16:24) He also taught, *"Take My yoke upon you and learn from Me, for I am gentle and lowly in heart, and you will find rest for your souls."* (Matt. 11:29) Jesus appointed the early apostles as leaders (or disciple makers) over the early church. You are prideful when you are a know-it-all and distance yourself from the body of Christ. (Note: You may distance yourself from the church because of woundedness, but that is a separate issue; here, I am merely addressing the arrogant person who thinks they know-it-all or can do-it-all on their own). You are clothed in humility when you deny yourself, take Christ's yoke upon your own shoulders, and walk meekly and humbly with Godly leaders on the path of discipleship.

11. **Ministry:** Jesus gave the 7 gifts of the Spirit to strengthen the church and reach out to the unbeliever (1 Cor. 12:8-9). But He wants you to stay humble and to use your God given gifts with the boundaries of grace He gives you (Rom. 12:3-8). You are prideful when you use your spiritual gift(s) to serve and to glorify yourself. You are clothed with humility when you use your gift(s) to serve the body of Christ— especially in secret, where no one but God hears or sees.

12. **Rewards:** Jesus loves to give rewards!! He said, *"For whoever exalts himself will be humbled, and he who humbles himself will be exalted"* (Luke 14:11). He will exalt you (reward you) in His time, in His way, both in this age and the age to come (Matt. 13:43; 1 Cor. 15:40-42; Dan. 12:2-3). Paul talked about God humbling Him, and this brought glory to his life (2 Cor. 12:9-10). You are prideful when you run from God's

leadership and His gentle hand of humility. <u>You are clothed with humility</u> when you allow God to promote, demote, and discipline you, all in His time and in His way. You can trust Him. His leadership is perfect, and His rewards will come in His timing.

HUMILITY: practical assignment…answer the questions accordingly.
GROUP QUESTION: discuss whichever question seems most important.

1. Read ([Philippians 2:5-7](#))

2. What does this scripture tell you about who God is?

3. What does this scripture tell you about what God thinks and feels about you?

4. What is your definition of humility?

5. What is your definition of pride?

6. What does it mean to be clothed in humility? (fill in the blanks; pg. 65) Therefore, through _____ prayer and meditation, you _____ to the image of God. You do this with God's gracious help by allowing God to confront _____ in your life, and becoming the person He is asking you to be. There are so many _____ when you do this, both now and in the age to come ([Lu. 14:11](#)).

Clothed in humility QUESTIONS (the answer(s) to the following questions can be found in the text above.)

1. **Jesus** (pg. 65/66): What is one example (from notes above) about how Jesus was humble?

2. **Word of God and the Holy Spirit** (pg. 66): According to the notes above, how are you clothed in humility with the Word of God and the Holy Spirit?

3. **Sin** (pg. 66): According to the notes above, how are you clothed in humility when dealing with your past sin?

4. **Sin (part 2)** (pg. 66/67): According to the notes above, how are you clothed in humility when sin of others.

5. **Chastening** (pg. 67): According to the notes above, how are you clothed in humility when you are being chastened by God?

6. **Finances** (pg. 67/68): According to the notes above, how are you clothed in humility in regard to your finances?

7. **Prayer** (pg. 68): According to the notes above, how are you clothed in humility as it pertains to your prayer life?

8. **Testimonies** (pg. 68): According to the notes above, how are you clothed in humility when sharing a testimony?

9. **Discipling others** (pg. 68/69): According to the notes above, how are you clothed in humility when you disciple others?

10. **Being discipled** (pg. 69): According to the notes above, how are you clothed in humility when you are being discipled?

11. **Ministry** (pg. 69): According to the notes above, how are you clothed in humility when ministering to the body of Christ?

12. **Rewards** (pg. 69/70): According to the notes above, how are you clothed in humility in regards to God rewarding you?

If you desire more humility in your life, then pray this prayer: (page 72)

Father, I understand that You are holy. You are sacred and set apart. Part of Your holiness—is Your humility—and You call me to be holy like You. Therefore, confront the pride in my life. When I read Your Word, open my eyes to areas where I am prideful, and conform me to walk humbly before You. I trust your leadership. Please reward me in Your timing. Let me become the fullness of the person that You intended me to be. Holy Spirit come, make me humble in Jesus Name.

ordinary people called to do extraordinary things

PRAYER #talk2God #textingGod
Pre-Foundation #8

"And when you pray do not use vain repetitions as the heathen do. For they think that they will be heard for their many words…In this manner, therefore pray: Our Father in Heaven…." (Matt. 6:8-9)

GOAL:
(Step #1) To understand God's heart for easy enjoyable prayer.

(Step #2) To build your prayer life day-by-day!

Prayer is the smartest phone. Prayer is what God the Father invented to talk to you. But the service is not free. Jesus willingly gave His life that you could have your own number, instantly giving you free face time with the Father. Prayer has high speed connection and the quality is out of this world—just ask the Holy Spirit. Prayer is very emotional; you get to feel what is on God's heart while He touches yours.

Let me ask you a question: how often do you talk to friends? How often do you talk to others? And on social media: how often do you "like" someone's picture or post? Really. Take a moment to come up with an answer. (I know, that was more than "a" question; bear with me.) Do you have your answer? Now, answer me these: How much time do you spending talking to God? When was the last time you prayed? You might say, "I pray." Or you might say, "Why should I pray? It doesn't work!" How do you know if prayer is effective or not? In order to answer this question we need to know God's heartfelt desires behind prayer.

The Father wants a family and Jesus desires a bride, while the Holy Spirit, who is God, is willing to instantly connect you to the private connection (the very private connection) called prayer. All throughout the gospels, Jesus taught us about prayer. He said, *"When you pray..."* (Matt. 6:5), NOT "If you pray...". He also said we should pray to our Father (you may have an issue with an earthly father, so call your Heavenly Father, and He will fill your heart with healing love). Also, Jesus teaches us when to pray by his own example: He got up early to pray, and He stayed up late to pray. Did you know? He desperately fought in the place of prayer! He sweat drops like blood (Luke 22:44) so He would not fall into temptation. He did this while His disciples slept. Jesus was willfully contending to bear the cross that you might be fully alive. Prayer is instant access to the very depth of the Father's deepest secrets, hidden in the mysterious chambers of His heart. Prayer lets you know that you're not alone, and that your Father always answers perfectly in His time and in His way. Prayer is instant access to the deepest love of your Heavenly Father, and to the highest love of His Son—the Beloved Bridegroom, Glorious King, and Just Judge. Prayer is not a means to the end—it is the end. You have the privilege to pray! You are invited to talk to God!

Texting God

God wants you to talk with Him because He loves you and wants an extremely close relationship with you. And when I say `close` the human mind is not powerful enough to even consider how close God wants to be in your life. You may say, "I am close to my friend", but God wants to be closer still. A husband may say, "I am close to my wife", but

God wants to be closer still. Even a mother may say, "I am close to my newborn child" (is there a closer bond than this?)—and yet the Holy Spirit tells us, *"Can a woman forget her nursing child, and not have compassion on the son of her womb? Surely they may forget, yet I will not forget you."* (Isaiah 49:15) The closeness of a friend...of a husband...of a mother...combine these together, and even then, you will hardly even begin to touch the sheer magnitude of how close God wants to be with you!

Now, where were we...oh yes...talking to God! It is very easy to talk with Him. Do you have a phone? If so, do you "text" your friends? Well…it is time to start "texting God"! That's right: it is time to start asking Him questions and getting answers (ha ha ha….no I don't have His phone number.) So, how do you "text God"? Do you just get out your phone and text God questions? No; texting God is the metaphor. Instead, get out a pen and paper and start to write. You can look at my example below to get a hint on how to "text God". The goal is to find out who God is and what He thinks and feels about you—to connect to His emotions for you.

In case you needed more proof of why you should "text God": Did you know that (3) texting is on the rise? Here's a stat for you: the average teenager sends 3,339 texts per month. That's more than six texts per waking hour. According to a new study from (4) Nielsen, our society has gone mad with texting, data usage, and app downloads. The number of texts being sent is increasing, especially among teenagers age 13 to 17. But what if we spent time texting God? What if you took that time to talk2God? What if you wrote back and forth with God? What would your heart look like? But don't take my word for it. Nicole was a university student, whose life was changed, while spending time texting God.

Last semester when I started going to Holy Clubs, I learned how precious our time with God is. I had been struggling with depression and suicidal thoughts this year. My thoughts were consumed with feeling purposeless, unwanted, and unloved. At one of our Holy Clubs, I had a huge breakthrough by "texting" God. God spoke clearly into my life by telling me what life meant to Him: **Nicole George; University student**.

Why take time to text God?

1. Firstly, God wants to spend time with you because He loves you.
2. Secondly, the Holy Spirit will teach you what you need to know to succeed, to overcome in the areas of your weakness, and to complete the God given desires of your heart.
3. Thirdly, you are called to *"go and make disciples"* (Matt. 28:19). If you know how to #talk2God, then your disciples will know how to #talk2God.

Example of texting God:

Directions: I like to start with a scripture and then talk2God, or "text God" back and forth. The two questions I use are:

1. What does this Scripture show me about You (God)?

2. What does this Scripture show me about what You (God) think and feel about me?

3. Then I try to summarize what be said with a builder sentence or main point.

EXAMPLE: "Our Father in heaven, Hallowed be Your name." (Matthew 6:9)

Question #1: "What does this Scripture show me about You (God)?"

Me: Father of Glory "What does this Scripture show me about You (God)?"

    Father: It shows that I am "your" Father and I am "our" Father

Me: What does that mean You are "our Father"?

Father: There is no one like Me; Father: Ask Me what that means.

Me: What does this mean?

    Father: I am not like your earthly Father.

Me: How can I trust You?

    Father: Wait and see. I will show you that I am good.

Me: Father, What is the "builder sentence"? Father: I am the good Father; worship Me!!

Builder sentence (or main point): You are a good Father; help me to believe You're a good Father.

After you text God, it is time to Pray: UP, IN, OUT

UP: (BELIEVE) What does this verse show me about who You (God) are? You grow in belief as you diligently seek the knowledge of God and then you declare the truth about Him, (i.e. who He is). Your ministry to God will allow God to increase in your heart and in the atmosphere around your city. He is enthroned in the praise of His people (Ps. 22:3). Also, He enjoys your devotion; you move His heart. When you minister to Him, He rewards your heart with more of Him. "Main point" prayer: Help me believe and give me revelation (ex. You are Holy, Holy, Holy…Lord God Almighty; Thank You, Holy God; help me to believe You are holy, give me revelation of your holiness).

IN: (BELIEVE) What does this verse show me about what You (God) think about me? You grow in belief as you minister back to God what He thinks about you. You must seek the truth about what God thinks and feels for you and then speak that truth into your heart so that you can grow in God, and become more like Christ. When you minister to God, He speaks tenderly back to you and touches your heart, filling your emotions with His truth. "Main point" prayer: Help me believe and help me obey (ex. You are Holy, and You love me so much, You made a way for me to be Holy just like you; Thank You, Father, for making me Holy; give me revelation of Your desire to make me holy like You. I will obey Your call for holiness; give me strength to obey Your call unto holiness).

OUT: How then shall I pray for my neighbor? "Main point" prayer: Jesus, help my neighbor believe and obey You. This is where you write down a summary prayer for those around you. Old Testament Prophets taught the people and then wrote down their prayers for others to declare. David ministered to God, prayed for Himself, and asked God for the people around Him (all the Psalms). Paul taught the people and wrote down the prayers that needed to be heard (Eph. 1:17-19).

ordinary people called to do extraordinary things

PRAYER: practical assignment…now you try it!!!
GROUP QUESTION: discuss whichever question seems most important.

1. Read (Matthew 6:9).

2. What does this scripture show me about You (God)?

3. What does this scripture show me about what You (God) think and feel about me?

4. How then shall I pray for my neighbor?

5. Then try to summarize what is said with a builder sentence or main point.

6. **Now put it all together and pray it back to God.** "Father, I know that You are _____ (answer for #2). And I know that you think and feel _____ (answer for #3). Set my heart to be like You. Fill me with love for you and for my neighbor. In the areas that I am weak, would you come and rescue me? Holy Spirit, fill me with Your presence even now. Teach me to pray. Give me the kind of prayer life that I know I need and one where I can talk2God freely day and night. Grip my heart with the things that grip yours. Teach me to pray."

ordinary people called to do extraordinary things

THE 10 LIES OF HOLINESS
Pre-Foundations #9

For God has not given us a spirit of fear, but of power and of love and of a sound mind. (2 Timothy 1:7)

GOAL

(**Step #1**) To read of the 10 lies of holiness.

(**Step #2**) To answer the invitation to walk holy!

TO BE or NOT TO BE HOLY — that is the question

God's character is holy and He joyfully calls you to be holy just like Him (1 Peter 1:15-16; Lev. 19:2-3). To "walk holy" is a divine invitation; holiness is not an option in the life of a Christian, or for only a select few "mighty" saints. Instead, it is the plan of God for your life. Holiness is not just a list of "what not to do". Instead, holiness is scriptural; God made provision (the ability to succeed) for your life in holiness. God does not call the qualified; He qualifies the called. So let's see if you believe any of these "10 lies about holiness". Wait! I know what you're thinking, "I don't have to read this. Or, I don't have time to read through this." Hummm...if you already think that, I imagine that you believe at least three of the lies below.

1. THE WORD "HOLY" DOESN'T MAKE ME FEEL GOOD:

People that do strange things make you feel uneasy, but the holiness of God is delightfully heavenly and brings you heartfelt eternal PEACE—NOW! Being holy is actually your calling and destiny. God is HOLY and Heaven sings about the holiness of God! You will feel GREAT as God fascinates you, empowering you to live holy (Rev. 4&5).

2. I WANT TO ENJOY LIFE AND HOLINESS IS A JOY KILLER:

Actually, God created joy—SIN is the real joy killer! Additionally, at His right hand are limitless pleasures evermore (Ps. 16:11). Truthfully, the closer you get to God the more you can experience joy. Why? Because you will see how much He enjoys you—yes, YOU—even with all your mistakes. And when you see how much He enjoys you, then you can enthusiastically enjoy yourself. And when you begin to enjoy yourself, you're free to enjoy other people—even the real annoying ones. How? The fruit of His Spirit inside you is JOY (Gal. 5:22)! And true joy is part of His plan for holiness.

3. I WANT TO LIVE A BALANCED LIFE! HOLINESS IS ONLY FOR EXTREME & WEIRD PEOPLE:

Extreme and weird people do extremely weird things, and "balanced" folks usually suffocate in a tiny box they created. Today, living a "balanced life" in this world may cause you to subtly fall, unsuspectedly sinking into the comfortable mire of lukewarmness. Did John the Baptist live a balanced life? Did Jesus live a balanced life? Does the fruit in your life resemble the early church? Do not ask how much you can get away with and still make it to Heaven! Instead ask, "How holy can I be in the grace of God?" God said, "I am holy", and you are to be holy like Him (1 Pt. 1:16). Pursuing holiness is not an OPTION in your Christian walk—it is God's only plan. Pursuing God's holiness, in His grace, creates the true (and perfect) balance in your life. (Side note: In fact, pursuing holiness not only affected me, but it significantly blessed my spouse and children…read more on my life and testimony.)

4. NO ONE CAN BE PERFECT…I WILL BE HOLY IN HEAVEN:

Yes, and NO! Waiting for God to make you holy in Heaven is like getting a paycheck each week, saving it in a lock box, choosing to waste away in a pig pen of poverty, and not cashing in until after you die. God called you to live "poor in spirit", not to have a "spirit of poverty". Paul goes further by saying you need to let go of the "lesser" things around you (the things that are not holy), and to pursue perfecting your holiness in the fear of the Lord (2 Cor. 6:11-2 Cor. 7:1). Furthermore, did you know that God—the Good Father—actually likes to give you rewards as you pursue Him? I know it's shocking, but it's true (read more about it here: Matt. 6:4, 6, 18; 16:27). Paul, who I think really understood God's reward system, goes on further to say that if you live holy today, causing yourself to glow with the light of God, then your hard work will be rewarded; you will be "brightly shining", wearing God's glory gear in the age to come (Matt. 13:43; 1 Cor. 15:40-42; Dan. 12:2-3).

5. I CAN'T AFFORD THE TIME IT TAKES TO BE HOLY:

You can't afford to waste your time on worthless things. I have had the distinct privilege of sitting with Godly and ungodly leaders before they die. And none of them ever said, "I really wish I had wasted more time." Purposeful time management for the sake of building yourself up in the things that are important to God will give you a holy life today, and treasure in the age to come. Your time is one of your most precious commodities (in fact, your time is a holy gift; Ecc. 6:3). Therefore, planning your time so as to spend 20 minutes a day doing Holy Clubs will significantly benefit your life. "I already have a quiet time," you may say. But what are you actually spending that time doing? When you take time to work on holiness, your whole life will be positively affected; you will live a healthier, happier, and holier life. This has actually been the biggest surprise to me in my pursuit of holiness. I found that when I spent time planning to live holy, I actually succeeded in continually pursuing holiness! Adversely, when I was not setting a plan to walk holy, my life quickly plummeted downhill.

6. I CAN'T BE HOLY! IT IS TOO HARD! I WOULDN'T EVEN KNOW WHERE TO BEGIN:

You're right! YOU can't be holy! But Christ IN YOU makes you holy, and Holy Clubs "FIRM FOUNDATIONS" will take you on a 24 step journey to walk out biblical holiness, building one step after another. Jesus died on the cross so that you could be holy. The Kindest Man alive—Jesus—has provided for you and is praying for your life of holiness right now ([2 Thess. 2:13](#)). BUT you have to access what God gave you. He did His part; now you must do yours. Pursuing a life of holiness is not the same as obtaining it; you are called to grow in a life of holiness. Christ in you—the hope of Glory—is making you a new creation ([2 Cor. 5:17](#)), and His mercy, grace, and truth will help get you there.

7. I GO TO CHURCH, READ MY BIBLE, PRAY WHEN I CAN, AND, WELL, I'M A GOOD ENOUGH PERSON. I WILL WAIT TO BE HOLY IN HEAVEN:

Who's standard are you comparing your "good" life to? Your own standard? The standard of the person at church that you know you're better than? Your judgment of your neighbor's standards? Only God, who called you to walk holy, has the perfect plan for your life. Yes you will be holy—glorified in Heaven—but God calls you to walk in holiness today ([1 Cor. 6:11](#)). Remember, the way you live in faithful service and holiness towards God today will dramatically affect your life in the age to come ([Matt. 25:23](#)).

8. I DON'T NEED TO BE HOLY; I HAVE GRACE:

Lol…that is like saying, "I have a car, but I don't need gas to drive it". God gave you His grace to live holy; grace is power to overcome sin and not a license to sin ([Rom. 6:14-23](#)).

9. HOLINESS IS JUST A LIST OF STRICT RULES, AND I AM FREE IN CHRIST. BESIDES, ONLY A FEW PEOPLE IN BIBLE HISTORY ARE HOLY:

Holiness is not what you don't do. Instead, it is what you actually do. Holiness is running the race, cooperating with grace, and becoming holy as He is holy. Jesus made you a—new creation. This gives you a fresh start and lifts you up after you have fallen down; simply staying in the race makes you holy ([Eph. 4:24](#)). God has called all of us to be holy and has given us 7 provisions for holiness: Jesus, the Cross, the Holy Spirit, His Blood, the Word, Faith & your Works. The Great Cloud of witnesses were not perfect and did not see God's promises fulfilled. BUT they stayed in the race and steadfastly cheer us on from the balcony of Heaven. Therefore, since you are surrounded but such a great cloud of witness, flee sin—stay in the race—by looking at Jesus! ([Heb. 12:1-2](#)).

10. I AM AFRAID OF FAILING! I HAVE TRIED TIME AND TIME AGAIN TO "GET MY LIFE TOGETHER"—BESIDES ONLY "PERFECT" PEOPLE ARE HOLY:

Seriously?!? Have you ever met a perfect person? God does not make perfect people. He made a perfect path for us to walk holy. Did you know perfect love casts out fear ([1 John 4:18](#))? And deliberate godly action kicks fear out of your heart ([Phil. 4:4-9](#)). Also, did you know that God can give you "self-control" so that you can safely stay steady serving saints ([Titus 1:7-9](#))? David was afraid and lacked self control; He ran fearfully from God's plan for his life into the enemy's camp. Unfortunately, he uncovered his lust and lack of self-control issue by staying up late, watching a woman bathe. HOWEVER, in God, he was an ordinary person called to do extraordinary things. And he continually pursued God's love and mercy with all his heart ([Psalm 27:4](#)). He messed up many times, but was not defined by his past mistakes. Likewise, you are an ordinary person that is called to do extraordinary things. The first time God testifies about David (and this is before his sins), He says that David was a man after God's own heart. We know this because the last thing written about him said that he was a man after God's own heart and that he did God's will ([Acts 13:22](#)). God does not call the "perfect" to live holy. Remember, He doesn't call the qualified; He qualifies the called.

ordinary people called to do extraordinary things

HOLY: practical assignment…now you try it!!!
GROUP QUESTION: discuss whichever question seems most important.

1. Read 1 Peter 1:15-16.

2. What does this scripture tell you about who God is?

3. What does this scripture tell you about what God thinks and feels about you?

4. Which one of the above lies did you believe the most?

5. What are the 3 lies you feel your generation believes?

6. What can you do to bring holiness to your generation?

7. **If you want to grow in holiness, then pray this prayer:** "Father, I acknowledge that You are holy and You have joyfully invited me to enter into Your holy plan also. Help me to see You as holy, high and lifted up, on Your holy Throne. Jesus, I understand that You are holy, and you have made me Holy—but I don't feel that way in all areas of my life. BUT, You died upon the cross and rose again that I might live. You are merciful; You don't give me what I deserve. So wash me clean from my sin and make me like you. Let Your Grace empower me to walk holy like You. Mark me as holy unto You. Set me apart for Your will. Mark my generation as holy to You. Set them apart to walk holy before You."

"It's not the person that makes one's life holy. It is the Gracious Father, who is holy, that invites us to be holy like Him; He makes you holy!" - Ben Atkinson

SALVATION
DO YOU WANT TO START YOUR NEW LIFE WITH CHRIST?

You can have powerful, personal, peace today through a relationship with Jesus Christ. Follow these steps one at a time and then pray the prayer at the end. The change will be in our heart.

Step 1 – The Father loves you. He desires a family!
The Bible says, "God so loved the world that He gave His one and only Son, Jesus Christ, that whoever believes in Him shall not perish, but have eternal life" ([John 3:16](#)). All you have to do is Believe in Jesus. Also, Jesus said, "I came that they may have life and have it abundantly"—a complete life, full of purpose ([John 10:10](#)). However, there is another important step...

Step 2 – People are sinful and our sin separates us from God.
We have all sinned. Each one of us have thought, said, or done something evil, which the Bible calls "sin". The Bible says, "All have sinned and fall short of the glory of God" ([Romans 3:23](#)). The wages (or debt) of our sin is death; the result of sin is our death; this is spiritual separation from God ([Romans 6:23](#)). But there is good news!

Step 3 – Our Heavenly Father sent His Son to pay the debt of your sin.
He paid for our sins!
Jesus willingly died in our place so we could have a relationship with God and be with Him forever. "But God demonstrates His own love toward us, in that while we were still sinners, Christ died for us."([Romans 5:8](#)). Thankfully, it didn't end with His death on the cross. The Father raised Christ from the dead, and Christ is the Kindest Man Alive! "For I delivered to you first of all that which I also received: that Christ died for our sins according to the Scriptures, and that He was buried, and that He rose again the third day according to the Scriptures,"([1 Corinthians 15:3-4](#)). Therefore, Jesus is the only TRUE way to God. Jesus said, "Jesus said to him, "I am the way, the truth, and the life. No one comes to the Father except through Me." ([John 14:6](#)). Do you want this?

Step 4 – Would you like to receive God's forgiveness?

There is NO WAY to earn salvation; we are saved by God's grace when we BELIEVE (have faith) in His Son, Jesus Christ! All you have to do is confess that you are a sinner; confess that Christ died for your sins, and ask for His forgiveness. Then turn from your sins; this is repentance. Jesus Christ personally knows you and loves you. What really matters to Him is the attitude of your heart, your honesty, and sincerity (God can see into our heart and thoughts). I suggest praying the following prayer to start the continue the journey—accept Christ as your Savior TODAY!

Step 5 - Pray this prayer

My Heavenly Father
"I confess that I'm a sinner, and I ask for Your forgiveness.
I believe Jesus Christ is Your Son, and He is the Way, The Truth, and the LIFE. I believe that He died for my sin and that You raised Him back to life again.
I want to trust Him as my Savior and follow Him day-by-day as my Lord. Guide my life and help me to do your will. I pray this prayer in faith; wash my heart clean in your mercy and empower me through your grace. In Jesus' name I pray, Amen."

If you just prayed this prayer, tell someone! Then email us at holyclubs@gmail.com and let us know that you just prayed the **"SALVATION PRAYER"**.

ordinary people called to do extraordinary things

24 FIRM FOUNDATIONS (pg. 90-161)

1. Texting God
2. Encounter God
3. Pray UP, IN, OUT
4. Ministry to God
5. 1st commandment
6. Obedience (Matt. 5,6,7)
7. Repent. Believe. Mercy. Grace
8. What is Holiness?
9. 7 Provisions for Holiness
10. Jesus: provision for holiness
11. Cross: provision for holiness
12. Holy Spirit: provision for holiness
13. Blood: provision for holiness
14. Word: provision for holiness
15. Faith and our Works: provisions for holiness
16. Grace #1
17. Grace #2
18. Grace #3
19. Name of God
20. Who is the Father?
21. Living Sacrifices: provision for holiness
22. Forgiveness: provision for holiness
23. Hebrews 12: race of holiness
24. Jesus: Just Judge, Bridegroom and King

ordinary people called to do extraordinary things

SCRIPTURE – You start with the Scripture as your door to encountering God the Father.

ENCOUNTER GOD (Go to www.holyclubs.com for a teaching called "Encountering God")

FIRST, read the Bible content around the scripture; settle your heart before God; then read the meditation verse again; say the scriptures over slowly. You do this to give your heart permission to focus on Jesus in the Scripture; you want to set your heart on God, and distance yourselves from distractions.

SECOND, close your eyes; Go to God; PRAY for the Holy Spirit to teach you all things; PRAY Holy Spirit guide me to the Truth. You do this to set yourselves and come closer to the Holy Spirit; you do not want to be content with just sensing the Holy Spirit's Presence. Instead, you want to go as close as you can to God. Pray for the Holy Spirit to teach you all things so that you are waiting upon Him and not your intellect.

THIRD, say the scripture slowly, pausing for God to reveal Himself—to reveal TRUTH. It takes God, the Holy Spirit, to reveal God; wait for the Holy Spirit to highlight a word or phrase in the verse.

FOURTH, answer the questions accordingly. REMEMBER talk to God, not just about Him.

TEXTING 3 QUESTIONS – when you text God start with these 3 questions:

1. What does this scripture show me about who YOU (God) are?
2. What does this scripture show me about what YOU (God) think about me?
3. How then shall I pray for my neighbor?

HOW TO TEXT GOD?
1. **Dialogue back and forth** – you want to write questions to God and allow God to respond.
2. **Write down** – you write down what you think God may be saying, you do not have to hear "exactly" with "BIG thunder" from Heaven. You write it down because this forces your heart to respond and connect with God at a deeper level.

BUILDER SENTENCE AS A PRAYER – God wants to talk to you. When you write your builder sentence (or the "main point" of your meditation) as a prayer, it will be in two parts:
1. **KNOW** – write down the knowledge of God; what He is showing you based on the scripture. (ex. "Our Father in Heaven"... He is a good Father)
2. **BELIEVE** – write down what He has showed you in the builder sentence, but turn the sentence into prayer. (Example of a "builder sentence" You are a good Father; open my eyes to see You; help me to believe you're a good Father).

EXAMPLE: "Our Father in heaven, Hallowed be Your name." (Matthew 6:9)

Question #1: "What does this scripture show me about You (God)?"
Me: Father of Glory "What does this scripture show me about You (God)?"
　　Father: It shows that I am "your" Father and I am "our" Father
Me: What does that mean You are "our Father"?
Father: There is no one like Me; **Father:** Ask Me what that means.
Me: What does this mean?
　　Father: I am not like your earthly Father.
Me: How can I trust You?
　　Father: Wait and see I will show you that I am good
Me: Father, What is the "builder sentence"? Father: I am the good Father worship Me!!

Builder sentence (or main point): You are a good Father; help me to believe You're a good Father.

"In this manner, therefore, pray: <u>Our Father in heaven</u>, Hallowed (Holy and Consecrated) be Your name. Your kingdom come. Your will be done…On earth as it is in heaven." ([Matt. 6:9-10](#))

ENCOUNTER GOD: FIRST read [Matt. 6:5-15](#); then read the above scripture over slowly. **SECOND,** close your eyes, Go to God, PRAY for the Holy Spirit to teach you all things, PRAY the Holy Spirit guide you into the Truth. **THIRD,** say the scripture slowly pausing for God to reveal Himself—to highlight a section of the Scripture. **FOURTH,** answer the questions accordingly. REMEMBER talk to God, not just about Him. Pray what you wrote: UP, IN, OUT.

UP – (BELIEVE) What does this verse show me about who You (God) are?

IN – (BELIEVE) What does this verse show me about what You (God) think about me?

OUT - How then shall I pray for my neighbor?

ENCOUNTERING GOD — FOUNDATION 2

THE HOLY SPIRIT IS GOD

John teaches, *"For there are three that bear witness in heaven: the Father, the Word, and the Holy Spirit; and these three are one"* (1 Jn. 5:7). Therefore, God is inside of you; Jesus promised that God would not leave you an orphan, but He would give you the Holy Spirit (Jn. 14:18). In addition, God is Righteous, He is "Right" in all His ways, and you must seek and follow His will and ways.

THE HOLY SPIRIT IS HOLY

The Holy Spirit is "Holy"—He is sacred and separateness—His Name and Character. You are called to be Holy like Him (1 Pt. 1:15). Paul taught, "Or do you not know that your body is the temple of the Holy Spirit who is in you, whom you have from God, and you are not your own?" (1 Cor. 6:19). Your body is the temple for God inside you. Therefore, you cannot stay in your sin and you must pursue holiness; the Holy Spirit makes you a "new creation" and provides power over your past life of sin; sin no longer has power over your walk in holiness (Rom. 6:10-14). Paul teaches that your unholy actions can grieve the Holy Spirit, "And do not grieve the Holy Spirit of God, by whom you were sealed for the day of redemption" (Eph. 4:30).

THE WORK OF THE HOLY SPIRIT

1. **NEAR:** The Holy Spirit is "near" you before your salvation to convict you of sin, righteousness and judgment. (John 16:8-11); He continues to convict you in your walk of holiness (1 Cor. 7:1)
2. **IN:** The Holy Spirit is "in" you when you are born again. (Rom. 8:9; 2 Cor. 1:22)

3. **ON:** The Holy Spirit comes "on" you as anointing to accomplish His will (Lu. 20:22; Acts 2:1-4)

BAPTISM OF HOLY SPIRIT
You are baptized in water for the remission of sin and baptized with the Holy Spirit and fire (Lu. 3:16). This may be simultaneously like Jesus' baptism (Matt. 3:16), or it may be two separate events like at Cornelius' house (Acts 10:44-48) and Paul at Ephesus (Acts 19:6).

THE HOLY SPIRIT HELPS IN OUR WEAKNESS (PRAYER LIFE)
Paul taught, "Likewise the Spirit also helps in our weaknesses. For we do not know what we should pray for as we ought, but the Spirit Himself makes intercession for us with groanings which cannot be uttered" (Rom. 8:26). Love God – Your prayer life to love God; fruit of the Spirit growing in your life (Gal. 5:22-23) (keep 1st comm. 1st place in your life; Matt. 22:34-40). Love neighbor – Your prayer life to love your neighbor as yourself (Matt. 22:34-40); the gifts of the Holy Spirit in you, while your hands are instruments of righteousness (1 Cor. 12:1-11).

ENCOUNTER GOD (practical steps; more at holyclubs.com)
FIRST, read the Bible content around the scripture; settle your heart before God; then read the meditation verse again; say the scriptures over slowly. You do this to give your heart permission to focus on Jesus in the Scripture; you want to set your heart on God, and distance yourselves from distractions.

SECOND, close your eyes; Go to God; PRAY for the Holy Spirit to teach you all things; PRAY Holy Spirit guide you to the Truth. You do this to set yourselves and come closer to the Holy Spirit; you do not want to be content with just sensing the Holy Spirit's Presence. Instead, you want to go as close as you can to God. Pray for the Holy Spirit to teach you all things so that you are waiting upon Him and not your intellect.

THIRD, say the scripture slowly pausing FOR GOD TO REVEAL HIMSELF— to reveal TRUTH. It takes God, the Holy Spirit, to reveal God; wait for the Holy Spirit to highlight a word or phrase in the verse.

FOURTH, answer the questions accordingly. REMEMBER TALK TO GOD, NOT JUST ABOUT HIM.

"For God so loved the world that He gave His only begotten Son, that whoever believes in Him should not perish but have everlasting life." (John 3:16)

ENCOUNTER GOD: **FIRST** read John 3:1-21; then, read the scripture above slowly. **SECOND,** close your eyes, Go to God, PRAY for the Holy Spirit to teach you all things, PRAY the Holy Spirit guide you to the Truth. **THIRD,** say the scripture slowly pausing for God to reveal Himself—to highlight a section of the scripture. **FOURTH,** answer the questions accordingly.

UP – (BELIEVE) What does this verse show me about who You (God) are?

IN – (BELIEVE) What does this verse show me about what You (God) think about me?

OUT - How then shall I pray for my neighbor?

ordinary people called to do extraordinary things

"But without faith it is impossible to please Him, for he who comes to God must believe that He is, and that He is a rewarder of those who diligently seek Him." (Heb. 11:6)

Believe: You believe God when you pray, read, and text the Word of God, which is abiding in Christ, so that Christ is formed in you. Most of all, you must grow in believing God; that He is and He is a Rewarder of those that diligently seek Him (Heb. 11:6); He is the ultimate Reward (Gen. 15:1).

Unbelief: Heb. 3:12 teaches that you must guard against unbelief. You guard against unbelief by growing in belief in God through the Word and Spirit; praying, "Lord increase my faith/belief" (Lu. 17:5). Your belief in God is increased as you exercise your heart in the Word and Spirit, while embracing godly painful challenges, allowing Christ to be formed in you.

He is / He is a Rewarder: (Heb. 11:6) You must grow in the Knowledge of God and belief that He is God, while you know that He will reward your diligent search for Him. God wants to give you the reward of a heart that is alive and vibrantly in love with Him, allowing you to do works of righteousness. In the same way, you must diligently seek Him; you have to do your part—talk to Him.

Believe: Passages of scripture that focus on promises to believe in God's Word declare truths such as God loves, forgives, leads, protects, and provides for us.

Obey: Passages of scripture that focus on exhortations to obey God's Word command us to walk in purity, bridle our speech, serve others, and the giving of our time and money to God.

Minister to God: You should bless, hallow, glory, honor, and worship God; All Heaven declares to God who He is; you can minister the truth, about Him, back to Him. Also, God enjoys when you bless His name (Ps. 72:19). David spent time meditating on the knowledge and Beauty of God (Ps. 27:4) then ministering to God, while setting up the house of prayer to minister songs to God (1 Chron. 6:31-32; 16:37). All the songs in the book of Revelation are prayed/sung "UP" to God.

Pray: UP, IN, OUT

UP: (BELIEVE) What does this verse show me about who You (God) are? You grow in belief as you diligently seek the knowledge of God and then you declare the truth about Him, (i.e. who He is). Your ministry to God will allow God to increase in your heart and in the atmosphere around your city. HE is enthroned in the praise of His people (Ps. 22:3). Also, He enjoys your devotion; you move His heart. When you minister to Him, He rewards your heart with more of Him. Help me believe and give me revelation: (ex. You are Holy, Holy, Holy…Lord God Almighty; Thank You, Holy God; help me to believe You are holy, give me revelation of your holiness).

IN: (BELIEVE) What does this verse show me about what You (God) think about me? You grow in belief as you minister back to God, what He thinks about you. You must seek the truth about what God thinks and feels for you and then speak that truth into your heart so that you can grow in God, and become more like Christ. When you minister to God, He speaks tenderly back to you and touches your heart, filling your emotions with His truth. Help me believe: (ex. You are Holy, and You love me so much, You made a way for me to be Holy just like you; Thank You, Father, for making me Holy; give me revelation of Your desire to make me holy like You. Help me Obey: I will obey Your call for holiness; give me strength to obey Your call unto holiness).

OUT: How then shall I pray for my neighbor? Jesus, help my neighbor believe and obey You. This is where you write down a summary prayer for those around you. Old Testament Prophets taught the people and then wrote down their prayers for others to declare. David ministered to God, prayed for Himself, and asked God for the people around Him (Psalms). Paul taught the people and wrote down the prayers that needed to be heard (Eph. 1:17-19).

"But without faith it is impossible to please Him, for he who comes to God must believe that He is, and that He is a rewarder of those who diligently seek Him." (Heb. 11:6)

ENCOUNTER GOD: FIRST read (Heb. 11:1-7); then, read the above scripture slowly. **SECOND,** close your eyes, Go to God, PRAY for the Holy Spirit to teach you all things, PRAY HE guide you to the Truth. **THIRD,** say the scripture slowly pausing for God to reveal Himself—to highlight a section of the scripture. **FOURTH,** answer the questions accordingly. REMEMBER talk to God, not just about Him.

UP – (BELIEVE) What does this verse show me about who You (God) are?

IN – (BELIEVE) What does this verse show me about what You (God) think about me?

OUT - How then shall I pray for my neighbor?

ordinary people called to do extraordinary things

MINISTER (def) – to serve, to wait on, to take care of, to contribute to, to attend to, to worship

Why Minister to God? God is surrounded with angels that minister to Him (Rev. 4-5); He called Israel to Minister to Him (Ex. 29:38-46); David ministered to Him (Ps. 27:4); Jesus highlighted those that ministered to His immediate needs (Mk. 14:3-9); Jesus asked the disciples to minister to Him by tarrying with Him for an hour (Matt. 26:40); He is calling us to minister to Him today (1 Peter 2:5; Rev. 1:6).

Ministry to God in Heaven: begins and ends with God. The Father, the Son, and the Spirit share their Glory (John 17) and then it touches the 4 living creatures, 24 elders, and myriads of angels. They witness His glory and holiness, and then they minister it back to Him (bowing down and singing), (Rev. 4-5).

Faithfully STAND: You are called to faithfully minister (fervently love God) even when others do not. "But the priests, the Levites, the sons of Zadok, who kept charge of My sanctuary they shall come near Me to minister to Me; and they shall stand before Me… (Ezekiel 44:15). Today, you can "stand before" God by keeping your heart alive (refreshed through the Word of God and revived by the Holy Spirit) as you exalt, bless, praise, and fervently STAND: sing and pray (consider this day and night in your city).

MINISTRY TO GOD: PRAYING UP, IN, OUT

Pray UP: minister UP to God (1st commandment love God) by serving God with prayer, words, songs, actions, etc. God loves you and you love God back.

Pray IN: minister IN your heart (2nd commandment love yourself) by speaking the truth about God (who He is and what HE thinks and feels) into your heart.

Pray OUT: Minister OUT to others (2nd commandment love people) by serving people through holy love with prayer, words, actions, etc. God loves you; you love God; love yourself; then love others.

EXAMPLES OF MINISTRY TO GOD

Moses' Tabernacle – the priest ministered UP to God (Ex. 29:38-46) with sacrifices and offerings, while they ministered IN through sacrifices and offerings for themselves (Heb. 7:27), and ministered OUT, standing between God and man; interceding for the people. Today, you pray: UP, IN, OUT.

David – built the Tabernacle of David where the priest ministered UP to God through song (1 Chron. 16) and at the same time he kept the temple sacrifices and offerings going (1 Chr. 16:39-40). He ministered IN by speaking the truth about God into his heart (Ps. 15:2) and writing the Psalms. He ministered OUT by creating and serving Israel as a warrior king and judge.

Simeon and Anna – Simeon was a priest ministering UP to God and looking for the Messiah (Lu. 2:25-35); Anna, ministered UP to God through prayer and fasting, looking for Jesus (Lu. 2:36-38).

JESUS' NEED - Mary of Bethany ministered to "Jesus' need" by pouring out her love by perfume (Mk. 14:3-9); Angels ministered to "Jesus' need" (Matt. 4:11), John ministered by leaning upon His chest (John 13:23); Jesus asked the disciples to minister to "His needs" for an hour, but they slept (Mk. 14:32-42).

New Testament Priests - Every individual Christian is a priest before God; priests to the extent that we minister UP—meditation, worship, intercession (1 Peter 2:5; Rev. 1:6). You minister IN—engaging with the Word of God, keeping your heart pure, growing in the fruit of the Holy Spirit; You minister OUT—loving people and serving them through the gifts of the Holy Spirit.

"But the priests…who kept charge of My sanctuary when the children of Israel went astray from Me, they shall come near Me to minister to Me; and they shall stand before…says the Lord God." (Eze. 44:15)

ENCOUNTER GOD: FIRST, read Eze. 44:15-19; then read the above scripture over slowly. **SECOND,** close your eyes, Go to God, PRAY for the Holy Spirit to teach you all things, PRAY for Holy Spirit to guide you into the Truth. **THIRD,** say the scripture slowly pausing FOR GOD TO REVEAL HIMSELF—to reveal TRUTH. **FOURTH,** answer the questions accordingly. REMEMBER TALK TO GOD, NOT JUST ABOUT HIM.

UP – What does this verse show me about who You (God) are?

IN – What does this verse show me about what You (God) think about me?

OUT - How then shall I pray for my neighbor?

THE LONGING TO BE WHOLEHEARTED—FIRST COMMANDMENT

God's ultimate eternal purpose for creation is to provide a family for Himself that includes faithful children for Himself and an equally yoked Bride for Jesus as His eternal companion. God promised to give Jesus an inheritance consisting of a people whom He fully possesses in love. I [the Father) will give You [Jesus] the nations for Your inheritance, and the ends of the earth for Your possession. (Ps. 2:8)

GOAL: To REST in knowing God and being loved by Him; God loves you and you love God; therefore, you are a successful "son or daughter" of the Father in Heaven.

Jesus said to him, 'You shall love the Lord your God with all your heart, with all your soul, and with all your mind.'(Matt. 22:37)

1. **Mandatory obedience:** God will cause all creation to obey Jesus (Phil. 2:9-11).
2. **Voluntary love:** God will raise up people who voluntarily choose to love Him.
3. **Equally yoked in love:** God wants you to love Him with all of your heart and mind because He loves you with all of His heart and mind (Jn. 15:9).
4. **Jesus prayed**: for His people to be supernaturally empowered to love Him with God's love. I declared...Your name ... that the love with which You loved Me may be in them. (Jn. 17:26)

5. **Bridal LOVE:** God's purpose is to select and train a Bride who would be prepared by voluntary love to reign with Jesus. The first commandment will be in first place in the Church when Jesus returns. For the marriage of the Lamb has come, and His wife has made herself ready. (Rev. 19:7)

6. **God's four-fold love:** Love from God, love to God, which overflows to love yourself, and to love others. You were created to be loved and to love.

7. **Jesus defined loving God:** as being deeply rooted in a spirit of obedience (Jn. 14:21; Deut. 6:1-9). You must love God on His terms (not on your terms). A core issue at the end of the age is whether you will define love on God's terms or by the humanistic culture that seeks love without reference or obedience to God's Word.

8. **Loving God is the first priority to God:** Jesus did not call it the first option, but a commandment. Jesus makes it clear that cultivating love for Him is the first emphasis of the Holy Spirit. Loving God is a glorious end in itself; however, it never ends with loving God, but always overflows with loving yourself and others (believers and unbelievers). You burn out when you lose the oil of intimacy; Jesus said you should be the 5 wise and not the 5 foolish—get oil (Matt. 25:1-13). The oil of intimacy is the first priority in living a watchful life (Matt. 24:42; 25:13).

9. **Loving God is the greatest commandment, calling, and lifestyle:** Loving God has the greatest impact on God's heart, your heart and others you impact, as well as being your greatest calling for your heart and in your ministry to others.

10. **Your spiritual identity:** as individuals is "I'm loved [by God] and I am a lover [of God]; therefore, I am successful." This is what you look like to God. You are not defined by your accomplishments. Jesus called the accomplished church back to the priority of love; "I have this against you, that you have left your first love." (Rev. 2:4)

11. **Bible Heroes of LOVE:** Mary sat at the feet of Jesus, and HE said she has chosen the "better part" (Lu. 10:42); David desired "one thing"—to gaze at the beauty of God and inquire in His Temple (Ps. 27:4); Daniel had a fiery passionate prayer life, and the angel said he was "beloved of Heaven" (Dan. 6:10; 10:11).

12. **We need revelation of the supremacy of the first commandment:** It is the standard of evaluation at the judgment seat of Christ…ASK, SEEK, KNOCK.

13. **Discipleship and LOVE:** do you pray for the ones you disciple to grow in God's LOVE first?

"…You shall love the Lord your God with all your heart, with all your soul, and with all your mind.' This is the first and great commandment." (Matt. 22:37)

ENCOUNTER GOD: FIRST, read Matt. 22:34-40; then read the above text slowly. **SECOND,** close your eyes, Go to God, PRAY for the Holy Spirit to teach you all things, PRAY for Holy Spirit to guide you into the Truth. **THIRD,** say the scripture slowly pausing for God to reveal Himself—to reveal TRUTH. **FOURTH,** answer the questions accordingly. REMEMBER talk to God, not just about Him.

UP – What does this verse show me about who You (God) are?

IN – What does this verse show me about what You (God) think about me?

OUT - How then shall I pray for my neighbor?

ordinary people called to do extraordinary things

"You shall be <u>perfect</u> [walk in all the light you receive] as your Father…is perfect." (Mt. 5:48)

HOLINESS AND OBEDIENCE: Jesus calls His people to make it their primary life goal to walk in perfect obedience by seeking to walk in all the light that the Spirit gives them. Pursuing this is not the same as attaining it. (Mt. 5:48)

THE BEATITUDES: Jesus calls us to live out the eight Beatitudes (Matt. 5:3-12) as we pursue 100-fold obedience (Mt. 5:48). The Beatitudes are like 8 beautiful flowers in the "garden of your heart" that God wants to fully blossom. They define love, godliness, and spiritual maturity and describe the kingdom lifestyle. Implied in all of God's commands is the promise of the enabling to walk out the command. *³Blessed are the <u>poor in spirit</u>, for theirs is the kingdom of heaven. ⁴Blessed are those who <u>mourn</u>, for they shall be comforted. ⁵Blessed are the <u>meek</u>, for they shall inherit the earth. ⁶Blessed are those who <u>hunger and thirst</u> for righteousness, for they shall be filled. ⁷Blessed are the <u>merciful</u>, for they shall obtain mercy. ⁸Blessed are the <u>pure</u> in heart, for they shall see God. ⁹Blessed are the <u>peacemakers</u>, for they shall be called sons of God. ¹⁰Blessed are those who are <u>persecuted</u> for righteousness' sake, for theirs is the kingdom of heaven.* (Mt. 5:3-10)

YOUR GARDEN: your heart is a garden; these 8 flowers must be cultivated as you "weed your garden" by <u>resisting 6 common temptations</u> (Mt. 5:21-48) and as you "water your garden" by <u>pursuing 5 kingdom activities</u> (Mt. 6:1-20).

RESISTING 6 COMMON TEMPTATIONS: Jesus highlighted 6 areas in which we wage war against sin in our hearts. They are anger (spirit of murder, Mt. 5:21-26), adultery (spirit of immorality, Mt. 5:27-30), disregarding the sanctity of marriage (disloyalty in relationships, Mt. 5:31-32), false commitments (spirit of manipulation to promote ourselves, Mt. 5:33-37), retaliation for personal inconveniences (spirit of revenge Mt. 5:38-42), and inactivity when mistreated (refusing active love, Mt. 5:43-47).

PURSUING 5 KINGDOM ACTIVITIES: Jesus described 5 activities that position your heart to receive more grace and strength as you consistently serve and give: charitable deeds, giving service and/or money (Mt. 6:1-4, 19-21), praying (Mt. 6:5-13), blessing your adversaries (fullness of forgiveness, Mt. 6:14-15; 5:44), and fasting (Mt. 6:16-18). These are disciplines that position your heart before God to receive more grace.

REWARDS OF OBEDIENCE: Jesus invites anyone and everyone to be great in His kingdom by walking in the Beatitudes. Whoever breaks one of the least of these commandments…shall be called least in the kingdom…whoever does and teaches them, he shall be called great in the kingdom. (Mt. 5:19). Without faith [confidence in God] it is impossible to please Him, for he who comes to God must believe that He is and that He is a rewarder of those who diligently seek Him. (Heb. 11:6)

PURSUING JESUS WITH CONFIDENCE IN HIS REWARDS AND PROVISION
Jesus addressed the necessity of pursuing wholehearted love and obedience to God with confidence—especially related to your finances and possessions (Mt. 6:20-34). He calls us to have confidence in His rewards (eternal and temporal; Mt. 6:20-24) and in His provision (Mt. 6:24-33).

TRIALS WILL COME: Your love and obedience will be tested in order to be proved genuine under pressure (Matt. 7:21-27). Will you persevere even when you face trials? The storms of pressures, the eschatological storm (2 Thes. 2:3-4), and the final judgment (1 Cor. 3:10-15) will show forth the truth of your life.

> *"…Therefore you shall be perfect, just as your Father in heaven is perfect."*
> *(Matthew 5:48)*

ENCOUNTER GOD: FIRST, read (Matt. 5:1-16, 43-48); then read the above scripture over slowly. **SECOND,** close your eyes, Go to God, PRAY for the Holy Spirit to teach you all things, PRAY for Holy Spirit to guide you into the Truth. **THIRD,** say the scripture slowly pausing for God to reveal Himself—to reveal TRUTH. **FOURTH, a**nswer the questions accordingly. REMEMBER talk to God, not just about Him.

UP – What does this verse show me about who You (God) are?

IN – What does this verse show me about what You (God) think about me?

OUT - How then shall I pray for my neighbor?

ordinary people called to do extraordinary things

"…In those days John the Baptist came preaching in the wilderness of Judea, and saying, "Repent, for the kingdom of heaven is at hand!" For this is he who was spoken of by the prophet Isaiah, saying: "The voice of one crying in the wilderness: 'Prepare the way of the Lord; make His paths straight.'" (Matt. 3:1-3)

Why is it important to REPENT.BELIEVE.WASHED IN MERCY. EMPOWERED BY GRACE?
Hebrews 6:1 declares you must first "repent" and then "believe" then the Lords washes you in Mercy.

LIFE Eternal or Perish: Jesus came that you may have life and life abundantly (Jn. 10:10). If you repent and follow Jesus then you will have a time of refreshing, which leads to LIFE Eternal; God's Mercy washes you, His Grace empowers you to live holy, and He chooses to bless you. If you do not repent and believe Jesus then you will perish (Lu. 13:1-9).

REPENT: to change one's mind for the better; to turn around; sorry enough to never do it again. Your repentance is initial salvation, or (1) justification; then daily (forgive us our sins Matt. 6:12) so that you can walk out your (2) life of holiness (2 Thess. 2:13); unto (3) glorification (Rom. 8:17; 18-25; 30).
   a. **You repent:** b/c God is God; He is Right; there are no others gods like Him.
   b. **You repent:** b/c God so loved the world; you change your ways b/c of God's love for you

c. **You repent:** b/c the Holy Spirit convicts you of sin then you must make a lifestyle change. **Mind:** conviction of your past sins; think of your sin from God's perspective; He is Righteous and the Just Judge that passes judgment on your sin (Rev. 19:11; 20:12, 13).**Mouth:** identify and confess your sin; this allows you to take responsibility of your sin; confessing your sin allows for MERCY & GRACE to flow in your life (1 John 1:9). **Motions (or Actions):** correct your past sins; you must change your works and actions from unrighteous to righteous (Luke 3:8); put in motion God's righteousness in your life.

BELIEVE/FAITH: you must believe (belief is a verb, while faith is a noun) God and be transformed by the renewing of your mind; you are not saved by repentance; instead, your saved when you believe in the kingdom of God and Lord Jesus Christ (Acts 28:31).
  a. **Believing in facts:** your faith must be based on the TRUTH of who God is and what He thinks and feels about you. You should not believe/faith in any other secular or humanistic idolatry.
  b. **Believing is personal:** your faith must be alive inside of you. Belief starts when you agree with God in your mind and His word comes alive—empowering your will; when you hear information and knowledge about God—and you agree with truth—then you have an active testimony, which brings life.
  c. **Believing is verbal:** You must confess with your mouth that Jesus is Lord and Savior; you declare this first to Him and then to others (Rom. 10:9-10).
  d. **Believing is practical:** When you believe in God then you will obey; believing is accepting and acting on those truths. Believing God affects your life of obedience; when you believe God in a living personal way than you can leave duty based-obedience and turn towards affection-based obedience (John 6:28-29; Acts 6:7).
  e. **Believing is continual:** You must continue on in believing God no matter how long it takes for the promises to be fulfilled (John 3:16; 20:31).

WASHED IN MERCY: God doesn't give you what you deserve; He is Merciful/Compassionate, desiring to wash you in Mercy. Jesus shows you mercy by paying the debt of your sin; He takes the debt of your sin, pardons you, and says go and sin no more (John 8:1-12).

EMPOWERED BY GRACE: God gives you what you do not deserve (Heb. 4:16); His GRACE is blessing and power to overcome sin; grace is not permission to tolerate and play with sin (Rom. 6:1-14).

"…In those days John the Baptist came preaching in the wilderness of Judea, and saying, "Repent, for the kingdom of heaven is at hand!" For this is he who was spoken of by the prophet Isaiah, saying: "The voice of one crying in the wilderness: 'Prepare the way of the Lord; make His paths straight.'" (Matt. 3:1-3)

ENCOUNTER GOD: FIRST, read Matt. 3:1-12; then read the above scripture over slowly. **SECOND,** close your eyes, Go to God, PRAY for the Holy Spirit to teach you all things, PRAY for Holy Spirit to guide you into the Truth. **THIRD,** say the scripture slowly pausing for God to reveal Himself—to reveal TRUTH. **FOURTH,** answer the questions accordingly. REMEMBER talk to God, not just about Him.

UP – What does this verse show me about who You (God) are?

IN – What does this verse show me about what You (God) think about me?

OUT - How then shall I pray for my neighbor?

"… 'You shall be holy, for I the Lord your God am holy. 'Every one of you shall revere his mother and his father, and keep My Sabbaths: I am the Lord your God."
(1 Peter 1:15-16; Lev. 19:2-3)

Holiness – God's character is Holy and He calls us to be Holy just like Him. Holiness is not an option to the life of a Christian, or for only a select few mighty saints. Instead, it is the plan of God for your life.

Holiness in the Bible – Holiness is not just lists of "don't do". Instead, holiness is found throughout the scriptures. Below is a list of words, from the Greek language, found in the New Testament, that explain holiness:

Holy – (Greek for holy is "Hagios": adj.) holy means: revered, sacred, and consecrated to God.

Saint – is the plural (more than one) of the adjective "holy"; saints means "holy ones".

Sanctify – is "to make saint" (saintly or holy) (i.e. sanctification; you are being sanctified now)

God is a Father – God is a Good Father; He is making good children that will be with Him forever. Therefore, you walk out holiness; honoring your Father in Heaven, and by honoring your mother and father on earth (when they walk out righteousness) (Lev. 19:2-3; Exo. 20:12; Mal. 1:6; 4:5-6).

God is both – God's character is Holy; you cannot separate God into the parts you "agree" with. You can get in error when you emphasize one attribute over another in an "unrighteous" way.

He is the uncreated God; He is righteousness; HE IS HOLY; His nature cannot be separated

    Holy fear of the Lord………..and…..…...Holy God will dwell with us forever
        Chastening Father…………and…………Adopting Father
            Righteous……………….and…………….Loving God
                Judgment……………and………………..Mercy
                    Wrath……………and……………………He is patient

HOLY Fear of the Lord: God is Holy and sin cannot dwell before Him; God is LIGHT and darkness can not dwell with Him; your sin cannot dwell in a God's holy presence (1 John 1:5).

HOLY God will dwell with you forever: God is Holy and LIGHT, and He wants to be with you forever (John 14:2-4); God made a way for you to be holy like Him through Jesus (John 15:1-8).

Chastening Father: God is Holy, He pours out His wrath against the unrighteousness and He chastens, or lovingly disciplines, the righteous (HE QUALIFIES YOU); the prodigal son realized he sinned against God; he repented before God then returned to honor his father, receiving father's love (Lu. 15:18; 21).

Adopting Father: God is gracious and filled with amazing adopting LOVE and He lavishes His love on the repentant heart; the good father welcomed back the prodigal son with open arms and restored him to the place of inheritance (Lu. 15:20-24).

Righteous: God is the Creator, He is Righteous in all He does; "For My thoughts are not your thoughts, Nor are your ways My ways,' says the Lord." (Isa. 55:8); God defines what is right and wrong and you can choose to follow. Sin is still sin even if everyone is doing it, while righteousness is still righteousness even if no one is doing it.

God is LOVE: He is love, but only He can define LOVE; For God so loved the world (Jn. 3:16) but you have to repent and turn to His Righteousness—and He will fill you with LOVE today & eternity.

God is Judgment: His Judgment is holy; He is the Just Judge of the Earth; His Judgment is right (Gen. 18:25). He is Just and will judge believers and non-believers (Mt. 25:31-46).

God is Merciful: God delights in showing Mercy. If we repent, and turn to God He will give us Mercy, and wipe away our sin (Matt. 9:13).

Wrath of God: Paul says, "For the wrath of God is revealed from heaven against all ungodliness and unrighteousness of men, who suppress the truth in unrighteousness," (Rom. 1:18)

God is Patient: God is patient (long-suffering), meaning He gives you many chances to do what is right; He judges the heart; He draws you to repentance; He is patient with the non-believer, who does not know any better; He is patient with the believer struggling with sin that wants to be free (Rom. 2:4).

"but as He who called you is holy, you also be holy in all your conduct, because it is written, "Be holy, for I am holy." (1 Peter 1:15-16)

ENCOUNTER GOD: FIRST, read 1 Peter 1:13-21; read the above text slowly. **SECOND,** close your eyes, Go to God, PRAY for the Holy Spirit to teach you all things, PRAY for Holy Spirit to guide you into the Truth. **THIRD,** say the scripture slowly pausing for God to reveal Himself—to reveal TRUTH. **FOURTH,** answer the questions accordingly. REMEMBER talk to God, not just about Him.

UP – What does this verse show me about who You (God) are?

IN – What does this verse show me about what You (God) think about me?

OUT - How then shall I pray for my neighbor?

ordinary people called to do extraordinary things

"As His divine power has given to us all things that pertain to life and godliness (holiness), through the knowledge of Him who called us by glory and virtue, by which have been given to us exceedingly great and precious promises, that through these you may be partakers of the divine nature, having escaped the corruption that is in the world through lust." (2 Peter 1:3-4)

Why Holiness? – God's character is Holy and He calls us to be Holy just like Him. Holiness is not an option to the life of a Christian, or for only a select few mighty saints. Instead, it is the plan of God for your life. Holiness is not just a list of "don't do". Instead, holiness is scriptural; God made provision (the ability to succeed) for your life in holiness. God does not call the qualified: He qualifies the called.

4 TRUTHS ABOUT WHY YOU SHOULD TRUST GOD'S PROVISION
Full provision in God's power – Access to your holiness has already been given to you through God's power. 2 Pt. 1:3 says God has given "all things" that are needed for our life of holiness.
Knowledge of God - Provision comes through <u>progressive</u> Knowledge of Him; searching, believing and confessing (1) who God is and (2) what He thinks about you. 2 Pt. 1:3 says "…through knowledge of Him [Jesus]…" we can be made holy.
Promises of God - Provision is in the promise that God gives us. 2 Pt. 1:4 says, "…given to us exceedingly great and precious promises, that through these you may be partakers of the divine nature (holiness)." God's promises are truth (promises found in the Word of

God and through revelation from the Holy Spirit), and you apply them to your life; His promises are "yes" and "amen" (2 Cor. 1:20)

Divine nature - As you believe and receive God's promises you will look more like God and less like the world. 2 Pt. 1:4 says, "...partakers of the divine nature (look like God)", which means you can escape "the corruption that is in the world through lust."

PROVISION FOR HOLINESS – Jesus calls us to be like Him and provided a way for us to do this:

Jesus Christ – The Father gives the provision of knowledge of HIMSELF through Jesus (2 Pt. 1:3), and He gives the provision of sanctification and redemption through Jesus (1 Cor. 1:2; 30); searching out knowledge about Jesus will give you super power to live holy today.

The Cross – (Jesus' sacrifice) God gave the provision of the power of the Cross, taking our sins away, if we are willing, "for by one offering God has perfected forever those who are being sanctified." (Heb. 10:14). The cross broke the power of sin in your life, and you can walk in FREEDOM; the sin that controls you can be broken because of the provision of the cross.

The Holy Spirit – The Holy Spirit is the ultimate power, and is your provision for holiness. He is the helper (John 14:26) who will sanctify you (power to make you holy today) (1 Cor. 6:11), and transform you into the fullness of Christ (Eph. 4:13). Holy Spirit helps us pray His will (Rom. 8:26-27)

The Blood of Jesus – The provision of the blood of Jesus separates us from our old, sinful past and makes us Holy. (Heb. 10:29; 13:12). The Blood of Jesus covers our past sins, which dragged us down, and has super power to strengthen us to soar high into a life of holiness.

The Word of God – The Word of God is provision for holiness in that His Word sanctifies you (John 17:17). Jesus, before He left earth, earnestly prayed to the Father, that the Word of God sanctify you. As you read your Bible, all the answers for your holiness are there. Don't just read the Word of God, let the Word of God read you—let His Word sanctify you; when in doubt, read your Bible.

It is important to note that the first 5 provisions are God's part, while the last 2 are your part. God does His part and then you must do your part.

Our Faith/Believe – The provision of "Faith/Believe" requires that you believe in God. You have to take a leap and trust (come into agreement) with the Father who has qualified (certified) your life of holiness (Col. 1:12).

Our Works – The provision of sanctification, through your works, is powerful; God gives you strength to live holy as you do the Biblical actions that express your faith in God (James 2:22-26) (i.e. works of repentance, that build our inner heart; works to build up the church).

"as His divine power has given to us all things that pertain to life and godliness (holiness), through the knowledge of Him who called us by glory and virtue, by which have been given to us exceedingly great and precious promises, that through these you may be partakers of the divine nature, having escaped the corruption that is in the world through lust." *(2 Peter 1:3-4)*

ENCOUNTER GOD: FIRST, read 2 Peter 1:1-4; read above text slowly. **SECOND,** close your eyes, Go to God, PRAY for the Holy Spirit to teach you all things, PRAY for Holy Spirit to guide you into the Truth. **THIRD,** say the scripture slowly pausing FOR GOD TO REVEAL HIMSELF—to reveal TRUTH. **FOURTH,** answer the questions accordingly. REMEMBER TALK TO GOD, NOT JUST ABOUT HIM.

UP – What does this verse show me about who You (God) are?

IN – What does this verse show me about what You (God) think about me?

OUT - How then shall I pray for my neighbor?

ordinary people called to do extraordinary things

JESUS: PROVISION FOR HOLINESS
FOUNDATION 10

*"...to those who are **sanctified in Christ Jesus**, called to be **saints**, with all who in every place call on the name of Jesus Christ our Lord,"* (1 Cor. 1:2, 30)

What is "Appropriation" for holiness – (appropriation def. taking something for your own use) Israel was given the "promised land", but they had to leave Egypt, follow God in the wilderness, follow the leadership of God, cross the Jordan, and take the land step by step; your life of holiness has been given to you by God, but you have to appropriate, or walk out, your life of holiness "step-by-step".

What is "provision" for holiness? – God's character is Holy and He calls us to be Holy just like Him. Holiness is not an option to the life of a Christian, or for only a select few mighty saints. Instead, it is the plan of God for your life. Holiness is not just a list of "don't do". Instead, holiness is scriptural; God made provision (the ability to succeed) for your life in holiness; you have to gain access to these.

TRUTHS ABOUT SANCTIFICATION PROCESS

A STORY AND DREAM ABOUT HOLINESS (holyclubs.com)

WHAT CAN WE LEARN FROM THE CHURCH AT CORINTH TODAY (holyclubs.com)

PROVISION FOR HOLINESS IN JESUS

Jesus calls us to be HOLY like Him and provided a way for us to do this:

JESUS CHRIST PROVIDES FOR YOUR SANCTIFICATION: (1 Cor. 1:2, 30) The Father has provided the bank account of "Jesus", which is all that you need, for your day and night sanctification process.

THE FATHER GIVES THE PROVISION of POWER FOR HOLINESS: The Father gives His divine power for you to walk a path of holiness, and you do not need any other source of strength to guide or bring you into freedom. (2 Pt. 1:3)

JESUS IS TRUTH, HE PROVIDES FOR YOUR SANCTIFICATION FROM WATERED DOWN CHRISTIANITY: (1 Cor. 2:2, 5) The church needs to understand the foundational teachings of Jesus and believe that they are truth above all else.

JESUS IS THE RESURRECTION AND LIFE; HE PROVIDES FOR SANCTIFICATION TO OVERCOME IMMORALITY: The Father raised Christ from the dead. This proves that Jesus was sinless and death could not hold on to Jesus (Acts 2:24). The same power that raised Jesus from the dead is available for us. The same power of God that made Jesus sinless is available for us; we are called to die to sin and then sin will not have power over us (Rom. 6:4).

JESUS PROVIDES FOR US TO LOVE OUR NEIGHBOR AND OVERCOME SELFISHNESS: Jesus showed the unselfish love of God the Father; He humbled Himself, becoming a man, dwelling in a human frame. He healed the sick, had compassion on the weak, was patient with humanity, washed the feet of the disciples, and sacrificed His own life that you may live. (1 Cor. 13:1-13)

JESUS IS THE GREAT INTERCESSOR; HIS INTERCESSION MAKES YOU HOLY: (Romans 8:34) You can gain confidence knowing that the Greatest intercessor is praying for you right now, and He loves you, and He is praying the Father's good will for you.

JESUS IS THE REDEEMER; HIS REDEMPTION MAKES YOU HOLY: (Eph. 1:4-7) Jesus has redeemed you, bought you from the debt of sin, and freed you into the newness of life.

Goals: Set a goal to search out Jesus as your primary source for holiness (pray for grace)

"...to those who are sanctified in Christ Jesus, called to be saints, with all who in every place call on the name of Jesus Christ our Lord," (1 Cor. 1:2)

ENCOUNTER GOD: FIRST read 1 Cor. 1:1-9; then read above verse over slowly. **SECOND,** close your eyes, Go to God, PRAY for the Holy Spirit to teach you all things, PRAY for Holy Spirit to guide you into the Truth. **THIRD,** say the scripture slowly pausing for God to reveal Himself—to reveal TRUTH. **FOURTH,** answer the questions accordingly. REMEMBER talk to God, not just about Him.

UP – What does this verse show me about who You (God) are?

IN – What does this verse show me about what You (God) think about me?

OUT - How then shall I pray for my neighbor?

"…For by one offering He has perfected forever those who are being sanctified." (Heb. 10:14)

Do you feel distant from God? The cross of Christ has the power to restore you to worship God; to love Him and be loved by Him. The cross reveals the character of God—His love and justice. He loves the lost sinner and His justice is perfect in your life. At the cross, those who turn to Him are delivered from the penalty of sin, and they are delivered from the power of sin. Likewise, the cross is the place where all the wounds of sin are healed; the cross is more powerful than your pain. If you suffer from ANY emotional problems—guilt, anxiety, depression, anger, etc.—there is healing in the cross of Christ. If you are going through tragedy or suffering, there is absolute healing peace as you meditate upon the cross—the lamb that was slain for you. You receive God's righteousness and favor because of what Jesus did on the cross, not because of your good works (Rom. 3:21-31). It is necessary to sincerely repent to receive God's saving grace.

WHAT HAS THE CROSS-DONE FOR YOU?

The gospel is the good news of salvation, about receiving God's RIGHTEOUSNESS (in three tenses)

Justification: our legal position—past tense, focused on your spirit (you have been saved)

Sanctification: our living condition—present tense, focused on your soul (you are being saved)

Glorification: our eternal exaltation—future tense, focused on your body (you will be saved)

THE CROSS - PROVISION FOR HOLINESS

Jesus calls us to be HOLY like Him and provided a way for us to do this through the Cross of Christ.

THE CROSS: (ONE OFFERING) PROVIDES FOR YOUR SANCTIFICATION (Heb. 10:14) The Father has provided the bank account of "CROSS", which is all that you need, for your day and night sanctification process. One offering – the Cross of Christ, is the perfect sacrifice, performed by the perfect Priest, with the power to: cleanse your sins, make you perfect, and sanctify you.

THE CROSS: "HAS PERFECTED FOREVER" - Has perfected – The Cross of Christ "has made us perfect", which means that His one offering, this one time act, "has"—past tense—set you free once and for all (Heb. 10:14). God's Love for you is everlasting. Therefore, your sanctification is—forever!

THE CROSS: HAS MADE A WAY FOR YOU TO "BE SANCTIFIED" - Being sanctified – This means you are "being made holy", and speaks of your daily fellowship with God on earth, and your position with God in the age to come. The scripture says, "…those who are being sanctified." Sanctification is NOT a one-time act, but a day and night choice; being made holy is a continual process; you have to appropriate, or access (you must take ownership of) step-by-step. (Heb. 10:14)

THE CROSS: MAKES YOUR CONSCIENCE HOLY – Hebrews 9:9; 10:2, 22 teaches that God wants to heal your conscience; God is a healer and a restorer. The cross has made your conscience clean; He has the desire and power to make your conscience eternally clean—has perfected your conscience, and He sanctifies your conscience daily by healing those areas the enemy tries to control.

THE CROSS REVEALED THE FATHER'S WILL FOR YOU TO BE SANCTIFIED The Cross revealed the Father's will for you to be sanctified. Hebrews 10:5-7 declares that the cross was the will of the Father and Jesus accepted the suffering of the cross—for you; the Father's plan is to make you holy.

THE POWER OF THE CROSS: BRINGS SANCTIFICATION AND UNITY - Eph. 2:14-18 Paul exhorts that the power of the cross will bring unity to the church, including unity between GOD fearing Jews and Gentiles.

THE CROSS: REVEALS YOUR WORTH – "...for the joy set before Him He endured the cross..." (Heb 12:1-2). You are so worth it; Jesus endured the cross because God first loved you and He enjoys you. Your relationship with God both now and in the age to come is special to God. The Father's investment in you is costly—because you're worth it! For God so loved you that He gave His only Son…that you might enjoy God forever (John 3:16).

"For by one offering He has perfected forever those who are being sanctified."
(Heb. 10:14)

ENCOUNTER GOD: FIRST, read Heb. 10:11-25; then read the above verse over slowly. **SECOND,** close your eyes, Go to God, PRAY for the Holy Spirit to teach you all things, PRAY for Holy Spirit to guide you into the Truth. **THIRD,** say the scripture slowly pausing FOR GOD TO REVEAL HIMSELF—to reveal TRUTH. **FOURTH,** answer the questions accordingly. REMEMBER TALK TO GOD, NOT JUST ABOUT HIM.

UP – What does this verse show me about who You (God) are?

IN – What does this verse show me about what You (God) think about me?

OUT - How then shall I pray for my neighbor?

ordinary people called to do extraordinary things

"And such were some of you…But you were washed, but you were sanctified, but you were justified in the name of the Lord Jesus and by the Spirit of our God." (1 Cor. 6:9-11)

THE HOLY SPIRIT IS GOD & HE IS RIGHT
John teaches, "For there are three that bear witness in heaven: the Father, the Word, and the Holy Spirit; and these three are one" (1 Jn. 5:7). Therefore, God is inside of you; Jesus promised that God would not leave the disciples as orphans, instead, He would give them the Holy Spirit (Jn. 14:18); Jesus gave the Holy Spirit as a gift to you. In addition, God is Righteous, He is "Right" in all His ways, and you must seek and follow His will and ways.

THE HOLY SPIRIT IS HOLY
The Holy Spirit is "Holy"—He is sacred and separateness—His Name and Character. You are called to be Holy like Him (1 Pt. 1:15). Paul taught, "Or do you not know that your body is the temple of the Holy Spirit who is in you, whom you have from God, and you are not your own?" (1 Cor. 6:19). Your body is the temple for God inside you. Therefore, you cannot stay in your sin and you must pursue holiness; the Holy Spirit makes you a "new creation" and provides power over your past life of sin; sin no longer has power over your walk in holiness (Rom. 6:10-14). Paul teaches that your unholy actions can grieve the Holy Spirit, "And do not grieve the Holy Spirit of God, by whom you were sealed for the day of redemption" (Eph. 4:30).

Holy Spirit - Provision for Holiness – Jesus calls us to be HOLY like Him and provided a way for us to do this through the Holy Spirit.

THE <u>WORK</u> OF THE HOLY SPIRIT
   a. **NEAR** – The Holy Spirit is "near" you before your salvation to convict you of sin, righteousness and judgment and to make God know; your are chosen for salvation through sanctification by the work of the Holy Spirit and your belief in the truth (2 Thess. 2:13; John 16:8-11)
   b. **IN** – The Holy Spirit is "in" you, the day you are born again. (Rom. 8:9; 2 Cor. 1:22); the Holy Spirit continues to convict you in your walk of holiness (1 Cor. 7:1)
   c. **ON** – The Holy Spirit comes "on" you in the future as anointing to accomplish His will, and to sanctify you in your walk of salvation; in most cases we have to ask and pray for this as the New Testament church did (Lu. 20:22; Acts 2:1-4)

"AND SUCH WERE SOME OF YOU..." – The church at Corinth was not made up of perfect super stars. Instead, God took broken people and made them saints; the fornicators, idolaters, adulterers, homosexuals and sodomites, nor thieves, nor covetous, nor drunkards, nor revilers, nor extortioners will inherit the kingdom of God. According to scripture the work of the Holy Spirit in you can be tracked:
   a. God choose you before you existed physically, from eternity (2 Thess. 2:13; Rev. 13:8; Jer. 1:5), b/c God so loved the world; He loved you and chose you before we existed physically).
   b. Holy Spirit revealed God to you (2 Thess. 2:13; 1 Cor. 12:3).
   c. Holy Spirit convicted you; NEAR you (until you repented and believed) (John 16:8-11).
   d. Holy Spirit is; IN you, at day one of your salvation (Rom. 8:9; 2 Cor. 1:22).
   e. Holy Spirit will baptize, and or anoint you; ON you (Lu. 20:22; Acts 2:1-4).
   f. Holy Spirit will sanctify you unto their complete salvation (walk of holiness) (1 Cor. 6:9-11).

SANCTIFICATION – The Holy Spirit is a provision of God that is power to sanctify you (to be made holy). You must appropriate (walk out day-by-day) this provision. The Cross-justifies us, making us righteous, and the Holy Spirit will administer the GRACE of God, which is power to walk in liberty as a "new creation" in Christ (2 Cor. 5:17; 2 Thess. 2:13).

"And such were some of you…But you were washed, but you were sanctified, but you were justified in the name of the Lord Jesus and by the Spirit of our God." (1 Cor. 6:9-11)

ENCOUNTER GOD: FIRST, read (1 Cor. 6:7-11); then read the above text slowly. **SECOND,** close your eyes, Go to God, PRAY for the Holy Spirit to teach you all things, PRAY for Holy Spirit to guide you into the Truth. **THIRD,** say the scripture slowly pausing for God to reveal Himself—to reveal TRUTH. **FOURTH,** answer the questions accordingly. REMEMBER talk to God, not just about Him.

UP – What does this verse show me about who You (God) are?

IN – What does this verse show me about what You (God) think about me?

OUT - How then shall I pray for my neighbor?

"the….elect according to the foreknowledge of God the Father, in sanctification of the Spirit, for obedience and sprinkling of the blood of Jesus Christ" ([1 Pt.1:2](#))

WHAT DOES THE BLOOD OF JESUS DO?
Everyone sins and your sin leads to death. But God made a way for your redemption—He is merciful and gracious. By faith believe the Holy Spirit administers the blood of Jesus ([Heb. 9:14](#)), which takes you from the realm and authority of satan unto the leadership of the Kingdom of God (separates you from your past sins; your sin leads to death). The blood is for you (redemption/pardon), to you (deliverance unto new creation), and makes you (alive forevermore/life eternal). Hindrances to faith: there is no unworthiness, ignorance or helplessness that can bring doubt and overpower His blood.

O.T. – In the Old Testament when you sinned, God provided a way for your redemption by animal sacrifice.

N.T. – In the New Testament when you sin, Jesus' blood redeems you. He is the perfect sacrifice; without sin; His blood is the most powerful blood; Jesus' blood has the power to cover ALL sin ([1 Jn. 1:7](#)).

Why does Jesus' blood have power? (PARDON—DELIVERANCE—ALIVE FOREVERMORE)
First, God said He put power in the blood and provided atonement (PARDON) for your sin which would be made by the blood ([Lev. 17:11,14](#)); God said it, so it is—TRUTH.
Second, LIFE is in the blood ([Lev. 17:11](#)); God put the life of a person, power to exist

physically, inside of your blood. Jesus' blood has the "Son of God" inside it (Acts 20:28); Jesus' blood has God inside it; therefore, it is dominant. He chose to take your sins. He did this by shedding His LIFE BLOOD and redeeming you, making you a new creation (DELIVERANCE) (1 Pt. 1:2). **Third,** by His blood He entered the most Holy Place (Heb. 10:19-22) and His blood still speaks/intercedes for you today (Heb. 12:22-24); He made a way for you to be (ALIVE FOREVERMORE); you will be a king and priest to God, reign with Jesus in bridal love and enjoy His pleasure, forever (Rev. 1:6; Rev. 19:7; Ps. 16:11).

Provision for Holiness in His Blood – Jesus calls you to be HOLY like Him; His Blood provides:

Pardons then Reconciles (Rom. 3:24-25): YOU MUST BELIEVE BY FAITH, as you repent, God's Blood blots out your sin forever; Heaven PARDONS and RECONCILES you to God; freeing you from sin and death, unto—enjoying God and being enjoyed by Him; you are now justified—righteous before God.

Cleansing (1 Jn. 1:7): Once you are justified, you may still feel "gross" or "like you still want to sin" on the inside. The blood has the power to cleanse your insides so you can enjoy the blessing of God today!

Sanctification (Heb. 13:12): God said, "be holy for I am holy". The blood grants you power to have a new life of sanctification; the old is gone and the new is come; His character becomes who you are.

The Priesthood (Eph. 2:3; Heb. 9:14; Ps. 65:4): The blood licenses you to stand as a priest who intercedes: loving/serving God and loving/serving people. You get to dwell in His presence (Eph. 2:5; Heb. 10:19-22), offer praise/thanksgiving unto God (Ps. 50:14; Heb. 13:15), and pray for others (Lu. 18:1-8).

Victory over satan (Rev. 12:11): The blood has defeated satan; he was finished at the cross and will be thrown out of Heaven (Rev. 12), bound for 1000 years (Rev. 20:2) and will be burned with fire (Rev. 20:10). Also, satan is defeated today according to your prayers (Dan.10:12).

LIFE forevermore (Heb. 10:19-22): The blood of Jesus saved you from death and made a way for you to be alive forever more. You are not just saved from something, BUT you are saved for something. Today, be a new creation—alive and renewed—in your heart, soul, mind, and strength; enjoying God the most you can today; serve the living God (Heb. 9:14-15). Also, in the age to come, you are set to be a priest and king, which means you will reign with Jesus in bridal love (Rev. 1:6; Rev. 19:7); enjoyable prayer is not a means to the end…it is the end; enjoying the pleasure of God forever (Ps. 16:11).

Communion: Today, you take communion to remind you of the blood of the new covenant (Jesus takes away our sins). There is blessing when you take of the communion cup of His blood (1 Cor. 10:16). Also, you are warned not to take the communion (the blood of Jesus) in an unworthy manner or you could become sick and/or die (1 Cor. 11:26-28).

"…how much more shall the blood of Christ, who through the eternal Spirit offered Himself without spot to God, cleanse your conscience from dead works to serve the living God?" (Heb. 9:14)

ENCOUNTER GOD: FIRST, read (Heb. 9:6-15); then read the above scripture over slowly. **SECOND,** close your eyes, Go to God, PRAY for the Holy Spirit to teach you all things, PRAY for Holy Spirit to guide you into the Truth. **THIRD,** say the scripture slowly pausing for God to reveal Himself—to reveal TRUTH. **FOURTH,** answer the questions accordingly. REMEMBER talk to God, not just about Him.

UP – What does this verse show me about who You (God) are?

IN – What does this verse show me about what You (God) think about me?

OUT - How then shall I pray for my neighbor?

ordinary people called to do extraordinary things

THE WORD IS PROVISION FOR HOLINESS
FOUNDATION 14

*"... I do not **pray** that You should take them **out of the world**, but that You should **keep them** from the evil one. They are **not of the world**, just as I am not of the world. **Sanctify them by Your truth. Your word is truth.**"* (John 17:15-17)

PRAY: Jesus prayed for you and He always prays the Father's will; The Father will answer Jesus.
WORLD: God's plan was to always sanctify you while you are living on earth (today).
NOT OF THE WORLD: Jesus was Holy, He lived in the world but not of the world; the world did not contaminate Him; you are commanded, and empowered by God, to live the same way—holy!
SANCTIFY: "to make saint". Jesus prayed that you would mature into holiness by the WORD.

The Word of God is alive and Active: God's word one of the agents in your provision for holiness. The writer of Hebrews taught that God's Word was alive and active (Heb. 4:12), which means His Word is the truth to transform you and it is the light to your path (Ps. 119:105) (today and in the age to come). It is important that you have a life plan to walk out our life of holiness.

<u>**Provision for Holiness in the WORD**</u> – Jesus calls us to be HOLY like Him and provided a way for us to do this according to the bank account of His Word.

THE WORD IS JESUS: (John 1:1-2) The Word is God; The Word is Jesus; The Word was pre-creation, He is the only Begotten of the Father; the Word is the Living

Expression of the Father's divine personality, who came in flesh, and made the Father accessible.

THE WORD IS TRUTH: (John 17:14-17) Jesus is the Word of God and He is Truth. Jesus prayed, "Sanctify them by Your truth. Your word is truth". God's word is truth and it never changes, while other "worldly truth(s)" change with culture and social change (Ps.119: 89; 160). God's word is truth, therefore, it is alive, which means His Word has the power to change you into His image.

THE WORD SANCTIFIES: Paul (2 Thess. 2:13) taught, "because God from the beginning chose you for salvation through sanctification by the Spirit and belief in the truth…" Holy Spirit is your Teacher and Guide into a deeper walk of sanctification; He speaks Truth (The Word), brings you to belief in the Truth, & empowers you to walk in Truth, which is holiness.

THE WORD IS INTIMACY: God is Love. God loves God and loves you the same way (Jn. 15:9). Jesus, the Living Word of God, expresses His love to the world and you (Jn. 3:16). His Word creates JOY and LOVE, as you follow His commandments (Jn. 15:12); His Word is the only pathway to experience TRUE LOVE and Jesus gave His life that you might experience His Love (Jn. 15:13). You must read His word, believe His word, and then His Holy Spirit bears witness to the Word of God by bringing His Love to life inside you (Jn. 16:13-15). Solomon expressed that God's through a song, "Kiss me with the kisses of your Word (SofS 1:2).

THE WORD IS LIKE WATER: Paul taught (Eph. 5:25-27), God's word sanctifies and cleanses us. God's word can clean you so that you become bright and shiny just like on your wedding day. His Word will cleanse your way when you take heed (grow in knowledge) and hide it in your heart (Ps. 119:9-11).

KNOW (WORD) BIBLE FOUNDATIONS AND PROMISES: The bible is rich in foundational teachings and promises that are yet to come. 2 Peter 1:4 taught that, "by which have been given to us exceedingly great and precious promises, that through these you may be partakers of the divine nature, having escaped the corruption that is in the world through lust". God's Word and His Spirit help to bring understanding (Ps. 119:130).

PLAN FOR THE WORD: you have a plan to pay your bills by the end of the month, and you have a plan for other areas of your life. You need a plan to read the bible: read the bible through; text God; pray read the bible; learn foundational teachings; learn end times.

"... I do not pray that You should take them out of the world, but that You should keep them from the evil one. They are not of the world, just as I am not of the world. Sanctify them by Your truth. Your word is truth." (John 17:15-17)

ENCOUNTER GOD: FIRST, read John 17; read the above text slowly. **SECOND,** close your eyes, Go to God, PRAY for the Holy Spirit to teach you all things, PRAY for Holy Spirit to guide you into the Truth. **THIRD,** say the scripture slowly pausing FOR GOD TO REVEAL HIMSELF—to reveal TRUTH. **FOURTH,** answer the questions accordingly. REMEMBER TALK TO GOD, NOT JUST ABOUT HIM.

UP – What does this verse show me about who You (God) are?

IN – What does this verse show me about what You (God) think about me?

OUT - How then shall I pray for my neighbor?

ordinary people called to do extraordinary things

"…But we are bound to give thanks to God always for you, brethren beloved by the Lord…God from the beginning chose you for salvation through sanctification by the Spirit and belief in the truth" (2 Thess. 2:13)

OUR FAITH/BELIEF: The provision of "Faith/Belief" requires that you believe in God. You have to take a leap and trust (come into agreement) with the Father who has qualified (certified) your life of holiness (Col. 1:12).
Your faith is like an Internet line: slow Internet speed (dial-up) decreases your ability to surf the net. In the same way "your faith" is the avenue for God's provision to flow into your life; your response to God's Word and Spirit is your obligation; God will not force you to believe His truth (what about this last sentence).
How do we BELIEVE in Truth: (1) agree that God is RIGHT(eous) **(2) s**eek the truth found in God's Word and Spirit **(3)** choose to believe (or have faith): believe in your mind, confess with your mouth **(4)** obey by expressing your faith in your actions (works that follow truth).
Rewards of our belief in Truth: First, your sins are forgiven allowing you to freely worship the Holy, Almighty God. **Second,** you are washed in Mercy and empowered by Grace (Heb. 4:16); then you walk in the inheritance of a child of God, who is being sanctified/to be made saint (Col. 1:12).

OUR WORKS: The provision of sanctification through your works is powerful. Faith and Actions: your faith and your actions must go hand in hand together; your faith without works is dead (James 2:22-26). Perfecting Holiness: Paul taught one of the provisions for holiness is found in the promises God has given us…therefore, we cleanse ourselves (2 Cor. 7:1). Also, Paul taught, "work out your own salvation with fear and trembling (Phil. 2:12-13). Our works can also be expressed in **7 practical ways:**

RHYTHM OF PRAYER: CONNECTING DAILY WITH GOD WHILE IMPACTING THE WORLD – Daniel prayed 3x a day since his youth. You're called to find a daily rhythm of prayer, connecting to God & praying His Kingdom come and will being done (Lu. 11:1-13).

FAST WEEKLY: POSITIONING OURSELVES TO FREELY RECEIVE MORE FROM GOD – When you fast, which is abstaining from foods, the Father who sees in secret will Himself reward you richly, and you can see this in 7 unique ways (Matt. 6:17-18).

LIVE HOLY: LIVING EXHILARATED IN THE PLEASURE OF LOVING GOD - Holiness equips you to enjoy life together with God. You must not approach it in a negative way; b/c holiness is a call to the superior pleasures of being exhilarated in Jesus (Ps. 16:11).

DO JUSTLY: BEING ZEALOUS FOR GOOD WORKS THAT EXALT JESUS (Titus 2:14) - You are all called to works of justice, be a lover of mercy, while draped with a spirit of humility (Micah 6:8).

LEAD SACRIFICIALLY WITH DILIGENCE: TAKING INITIATIVE TO MINISTER TO OTHERS: can take initiative to diligently serve, support, and/or lead in practical ways in ministries like weekly holy clubs (prayer, outreach, and discipleship) (Rom. 12:6-8).

GIVE EXTRAVAGANTLY: THE JOY OF FINANCIAL POWER ENCOUNTERS – Giving our tithe and also sowing into prayer, giving to acts of justice, and giving to fulfill the great commission both locally and internationally (Mal. 3:10; Matt. 6:3-4).

SPEAK BOLDLY: BEING A FAITHFUL WITNESS - Jesus is the Faithful witness of the truth (Rev. 1:5). He did not hold back from speaking truths that were unpopular. You are called to boldly declare who God is, how to follow His ways, and share what He is doing (Jn. 18:37).

ordinary people called to do extraordinary things

"...But we are bound to give thanks to God always for you, brethren beloved by the Lord...God from the beginning chose you for salvation through sanctification by the Spirit and belief in the truth" (2 Thess. 2:13)

ENCOUNTER GOD: FIRST, read 2 Thess. 2:13-17; then read 2 Thess. 2:13 over slowly. **SECOND,** close your eyes, Go to God, PRAY for the Holy Spirit to teach you all things, PRAY for Holy Spirit to guide you into the Truth. **THIRD,** say the scripture slowly pausing FOR GOD TO REVEAL HIMSELF—to reveal TRUTH. **FOURTH,** answer the questions accordingly. REMEMBER TALK TO GOD, NOT JUST ABOUT HIM.

UP – What does this verse show me about who You (God) are?

IN – What does this verse show me about what You (God) think about me?

OUT - How then shall I pray for my neighbor?

GRACE: KNOW [PT. 1] FOUNDATION 16

"… Knowing that Christ, having been raised from the dead, dies no more. Death no longer has dominion over Him (sins of this world). For the death that He died, He died to sin once for all; but the life that He lives, He lives to God (The Father) Likewise you also, reckon yourselves to be dead indeed to sin, but alive (New Creation) to God in Christ Jesus our Lord." (Rom. 6:9-11)

New Creation – The Father gives you His Resurrection Power (Grace) "to be alive" 2 Cor. 5:17 (see below…)

Mercy – Mercy is NOT getting what you deserve (forgiveness; washed clean from your past). God gives you His loving-kindness even when you don't deserve it; When you sin and then repent, God gives you mercy by NOT giving you what you deserve, which is His wrath.

Grace - Grace is RECEIVING what you do not deserve (impartation of something positive; blessings; God's power that enables you to obey Him). Grace inspires you to repent or to come into agreement (realignment) with God's heart (Rom. 5:20-21; Rom. 6:14-19); Grace is not (1) seeking to earn God's love and forgiveness; (2) half-hearted response to receiving God's grace, which is permission to keep sinning (Rom. 6:1-2).

Resurrection Power- The Father raised Christ from the dead. In the same way union with Christ in baptism allows your burial and resurrection with Him. Paul says, "For if we have been united together in the likeness of His death, certainly we also shall be in the likeness of His resurrection" (Rom. 6:5); When Jesus came out of the baptismal water He was made alive; so you are made alive at your baptism. The Father "raised" Jesus from the dead—Resurrection Power; in the same way He imparts "new (newness of) life" to believers. Walking in "newness" (a new kind) "of life" shows outwardly that the believer has received new life (2 Cor. 5:17).

ROMANS 6
LEGAL POSITION – Rom. 6:1-10: Our legal position (what you received in Jesus through the Cross) you are dead to the reign of sin (v. 2); you are free from the power of sin; you still have "sinful desires" but the power/control is gone. So, you access the grace of God to live "alive in God" (when you are saved (justified) then you are a legal "child of God"; when you have a state license you can legally drive).
COOPERATE WITH GRACE – Rom. 6:11-13: Three principles to help you walk/alive in Grace: KNOW, RESIST, PURSUE.
OUR LIVING CONDITION - Romans 6:15-23: what He requires you to do to grow in love; what you experience as you cooperate with grace.

GRACE (Part #1) KNOW GOD'S TRUTH (Rom. 6:11) - knowing the truth (faith)
KNOW GOD'S TRUTH: Know who you are in Christ. To "reckon yourself" is to consider, see yourself as God sees you; Then you must contend, with Grace, to believe, or "knowing truth" You must daily search out these two questions: **(1)** who is God? **(2)** What does He think and feel about you?

KNOW: Dead indeed to sin – THE POWER OF SIN OVER YOU IS DEAD; Jesus defeated 'sin', so that you would also defeat the sin in your life. Your past sin is dead! The sin done to you is dead! The strangle hold of guilt, shame, and condemnation is dead (The devil tries to lie to you everyday saying the things that Christ put to 'death' have power over you; he tries to take you away from your 1st commandment inheritance and 2nd commandment call (happy heart, singing soul, magnificent mind, and steady strength).

KNOW: Alive to God (New Creation) – The Father gives you His Resurrection Power "to be alive" & "to enjoy life"; "new creation" (Rom. 6:4; 1 Cor. 6:12-14); When you are alive to God you received: a new position [righteous before God in heaven, being sanctified on earth, and glorified with God in the age to come], new power [power to love God, love ourselves and others, while overcoming sin], new nature [you are a new creation: heart, soul, mind and strength], new insights [wisdom, revelation, and understanding], and new destiny [instantly transformed to walk in the provision, inheritance, and destiny as a child of God]. This is holiness—you walking ALIVE with God! Holiness is not what you "don't do" Holiness is what you "do, do"—be alive in God.

"... Knowing that Christ, having been raised from the dead, dies no more. Death no longer has dominion over Him (sins of this world). For the death that He died, He died to sin once for all; but the life that He lives, He lives to God (The Father) Likewise you also, reckon yourselves to be dead indeed to sin, but alive (New Creation) to God in Christ Jesus our Lord." (Rom. 6:9-11)

ENCOUNTER GOD: FIRST, read Rom. 6; read Rom. 6:9-11 slowly. **SECOND,** close your eyes, Go to God, PRAY for the Holy Spirit to teach you all things, PRAY for Holy Spirit to guide you into the Truth. **THIRD,** say the scripture slowly pausing for God to reveal Himself—to reveal TRUTH. **FOURTH,** answer the questions accordingly. REMEMBER talk to God, not just about Him.

UP – What does this verse show me about who You (God) are?

IN – What does this verse show me about what You (God) think about me?

OUT - How then shall I pray for my neighbor?

"...Likewise you also, reckon yourselves to be dead indeed to sin, but alive to God in Christ Jesus our Lord. Therefore do not let sin reign in your mortal body, that you should obey it in its lusts.. And do not present your members as instruments of unrighteousness to sin..." (Rom. 6:12-13)

REVIEW

Alive to God – This means "to be alive" & "to enjoy life"; "new creation"; literally, God does not want you to live tormented by sin. Instead, He provides you with His GRACE to resist sin and become the man or woman He created you to be. When you are alive to God you received a new position, new power, new nature, new insights, and new destiny (see Firm Foundations #16).

New Creation ALIVE – God did not just save you from something—He saved you for something—to be a new creation, an "alive creation". Paul say, "Therefore, if anyone is in Christ, the new creation has come: The old has gone, the new is here! (2 Cor. 5:17)" Jesus did not go to the cross so that you would "just be saved" and have a blobby, depressed anxious life; satan tries to keep you in your old life, while God's grace is working to significantly transform your heart, soul, mind and strength into a new creation.

Romans 6

LEGAL POSITION – Rom. 6:1-10: Our legal position (what you received in Jesus through the Cross) you are dead to the reign of sin (v. 2); you are free from the power of sin; you still have "sinful desires" but the power/control is gone. Therefore, you access the grace of God to live "alive in God".
COOPERATE WITH GRACE – Rom. 6:11-13: Three principles to help you walk/alive in Grace: KNOW GOD'S TRUTH, RESIST SIN AND SATAN, and PURSUE GOD AND PEOPLE.
OUR LIVING CONDITION - Romans 6:15-23: what you experience as you cooperate with grace.

GRACE (Part #2) RESIST SIN AND SATAN (Rom. 6:12)

Resisting Principle (Rom. 6:12-13): We resist sin, Satan, and sin-provoking circumstances. "Therefore <u>do not let sin reign</u> in your mortal body, that you should obey it in its lusts. And <u>do not present your members</u> as instruments of unrighteousness to sin… (Rom. 6:12-13)

Do not let sin reign in your body: You resist sin by denying fleshly lusts that war against you (1 Pet. 2:11). Jesus emphasized the need for self-denial (Mt. 16:24). Grace is like a sleek sharp sword; grab hold of grace and slice sinful desires that seek to devastate your life (this is "resting" in grace). You can present your members: talents, time, money, heart, soul, mind, strengths (eyes, ears, hands, etc.) to God; you ask God to train and allow you to act and work in righteousness. Paul teaches, "The <u>grace</u> of God…has appeared to all men, <u>teaching</u> us that, <u>denying ungodliness</u> and worldly lusts, we should <u>live soberly</u>, righteously, and godly…" (Titus 2:11-12).

Do not present your members to sin: We must refuse circumstances that inflame sinful desires. We do not go to places, buy items, or look at or talk about that which stirs up sinful passions. The battle for sin starts with our desires. Our evil desires calls out to unite in depravity with darkness (James 1:14-15). This is the battle! You must resist the battle in your mind. Why? How? Why, Jesus died and rose again—so that you could be alive; His plan is not for you to continually struggle every day. How, you resist the urges by accessing God's Grace.

RESIST – When an evil desire rises inside or me I stop and say, "Holy Spirit, help me to resist_____, give me GRACE to overcome. Then I wait for the promise of the Holy Spirit, my Helper, to come with tangible power to help me to not sin. Keep asking.

ordinary people called to do extraordinary things

"...Therefore do not let sin reign in your mortal body, that you should obey it in its lusts. And do not present your members as instruments of unrighteousness to sin, but present yourselves to God as being alive from the dead, and your members as instruments of righteousness to God." (Rom. 6:12-13)

ENCOUNTER GOD: FIRST, read Rom. 6; then read Rom. 6:12-13 slowly. **SECOND,** close your eyes, Go to God, PRAY for the Holy Spirit to teach you all things, PRAY for Holy Spirit to guide you into the Truth. **THIRD,** say the scripture slowly pausing FOR GOD TO REVEAL HIMSELF—to reveal TRUTH. **FOURTH,** answer the questions accordingly. REMEMBER TALK TO GOD, NOT JUST ABOUT HIM.

UP – What does this verse show me about who You (God) are?

IN – What does this verse show me about what You (God) think about me?

OUT - How then shall I pray for my neighbor?

ordinary people called to do extraordinary things

"...Likewise you also, reckon yourselves to be dead indeed to sin, but alive to God in Christ Jesus our Lord. Therefore do not let sin reign in your mortal body, that you should obey it in its lusts. And do not present your members as instruments of unrighteousness to sin, but present yourselves to God as being alive from the dead, and your members as instruments of righteousness to God." (Rom. 6:11-13)

REVIEW

New Creation ALIVE to God – This means "to be alive" & "to enjoy life"; "new creation"; literally, God does not want you to live tormented by sin. Instead, He provides you with His GRACE to resist sin and become the man or woman He created you to be. When you became alive to God, you received a new position, new power, new nature, new insights, and new destiny (see Firm Foundation 16&17). Paul taught, "...be renewed in the spirit of your mind, and that you put on the new man which was created according to God, in true righteousness and holiness." (Eph. 4:17-23)

3 Distortions of God's Grace:

The Legalistic believer - seeks to earn God's love and favor by your stellar obedience, your devotion to God earns your righteousness and His love, forgiveness, and commitment.

The Compromising believer – seeks teachers and scriptures to validate a lifestyle that allows you to neglect the call to love, seek, and obey Jesus with all your strength.

The Confused believer – may be sincere, but is easily swayed by the last argument heard; tossed by various waves of doctrine (Eph. 4:14-15). The simple remedy is to be grounded in the Word of God.

GRACE (Part #3) PURSUE GOD & PEOPLE (LOVE)

Pursuing Principle – You pursue relating to and serving (1) God and (2) people with love. But present yourselves to God as being alive from the dead, and your members [your talents, time, money, abilities, eyes, ears, hands, etc.] as instruments of righteousness to God. (Rom. 6:13b)

Present yourselves to God - Your life's goal must be to make the 1st commandment 1st place in your life by seeking to know, love, and please God in a personal and wholehearted way. Your essential daily task—cultivating intimacy with God—just like you take time to eat, sleep, go to school and work.

Present your members as instruments of righteousness - This speaks of loving and serving people (family, church, and nations) in righteousness (more than just usefulness). You are called to do the 2nd commandment (love and serve people) so that you grow in wholeness of love/life as Paul teaches, "till we all come to the unity of the faith and of the knowledge of the Son of God, to a perfect man, to the measure of the stature of the fullness of Christ;" (Eph. 4:13).

What makes pursuing hard? – 2 problems arise. **Problem #1 God** – as you grow in love with God, you find out more about God and yourself that may be offensive to your mind. **Problem #2 People** - as you grow in love with people, you find out things about yourself and others that will make you want to run. You must know truth, resist darkness, and pursue God and people. You pursue loving God and people as you resist sin, satan, and sin-provoking circumstances in the context of knowing who God is and what He thinks and feels about you (this is why you text God questions 1 and 2). You are alive in Christ and God loves/enjoys you (you have to know the truth about God's heart as a Father and Bridegroom). None of these principles can be omitted. Some people resist sin and pursue God without knowing who they are in Christ, while others pursue God at worship/teaching/prayer meetings without pursuing people or resisting sin.

PRAYER – *God give me grace to pursue Loving You and people on purpose!*

"...Therefore do not let sin reign in your mortal body, that you should obey it in its lusts. And do not present your members as instruments of unrighteousness to sin, but present yourselves to God as being alive from the dead, and your members as instruments of righteousness to God." (Rom. 6:12-13)

ENCOUNTER GOD: FIRST, read Rom. 6; then read Rom. 6:12-13 slowly. **SECOND,** close your eyes, Go to God, PRAY for the Holy Spirit to teach you all things, PRAY for Holy Spirit to guide you into the Truth. **THIRD,** say the scripture slowly pausing FOR GOD TO REVEAL HIMSELF—to reveal TRUTH. **FOURTH,** answer the questions accordingly. REMEMBER TALK TO GOD, NOT JUST ABOUT HIM.

UP – What does this verse show me about who You (God) are?

IN – What does this verse show me about what You (God) think about me?

OUT - How then shall I pray for my neighbor?

ordinary people called to do extraordinary things

"__The Lord, the Lord God__ (Jehovah = "the existing One") merciful and gracious, longsuffering, and abounding in goodness and truth, keeping mercy for thousands, forgiving iniquity and transgression and sin, by no means clearing the guilty, visiting the iniquity of the fathers upon the children and the children's children to the third and the fourth generation." (Ex. 34:5-7)

WHY IS THE NAME OF GOD IMPORTANT?

His NAME is who He is – Your name identifies you with your family, culture and part of your story. God's Name declares His nature, character and HOLINESS; be holy as I am HOLY. Therefore, when God declares His name, He is showing who He is, what He thinks and feels about you, and what He wants to do on your behalf.

Jesus last prayer was about God's Name – In John 17 Jesus prayed 4x about the name of God. Jesus in the flesh Jesus was a living example of the Fathers NAME; Jesus asked that the disciples would be kept by the Father's NAME; Then Jesus said, I have declared Your NAME and will declare it, so that the disciples will grow in love. You must search out the NAME Of God to grow in HOLINESS.

PROVISION FOR HOLINESS IN HIS NAME – Jesus calls us to be HOLY like Him and provided a way for us to do this:

THE LORD, THE LORD GOD - (Jehovah = "the existing One") He existed before! He is the God who was, and is and is to come. God is Supreme on His Throne and nothing is above Him. His LOVE is Supreme, His HOLY Throne is Supreme, His GOVERNMENT is Supreme. Also, He is the Covenant keeping God (Deut. 7:9)

MERCIFUL – Compassionate towards you; Through His MERCY He loves and enjoys you even in your weakness He will wash you clean of guilt and condemnation to the humble and repentant—He makes NEW CREATIONS (2 Cor. 5:17).

GRACIOUS – GOD LOVES YOU, He will give you GRACE, bless you, and give you power to overcome sin and walk righteous, even when You don't deserve it (to those that are humble and repentant of their sin) —He makes NEW CREATIONS (2 Cor. 5:17).

LONG-SUFFERING – Patient and slow to anger; He is our Father, and He is slow to anger towards you; God the Father is faithful to you even in the your continual weakness; Through His MERCY He loves and enjoys you even in your weakness, while He gives GRACE to overcome sin.

ABOUNDING IN GOODNESS AND TRUTH – Goodness (kindness and faithfulness) Truth (sureness, reliability; His word is Right); Your Father has more goodness and Truth —for you—then you can imagine; The devil is limited in His attack towards you, BUT God the good Father is the creator of goodness and truth—His affections are towards you —and nothing can take that away.

KEEPING MERCY FOR THOUSANDS – for 1000's of generations, generation after generation, the Lord will give His people Mercy (He will wash away our guilt, shame, and condemnation even when we do not deserve) Mercy and compassion towards us are new every morning (Lam. 3:22-23). Note this in context of the 10 commandments (2nd commandment); you shall not make or carve an image, making for yourself an idol to worship (Exo. 20:4-6).

FORGIVING INIQUITY AND TRANSGRESSION AND SIN – God will Forgive (to lift, bear up, carry, take) our iniquity (perversity, depravity, guilt or punishment of iniquity) and Transgression (rebellion against God, nations and other people)

BY NO MEANS CLEARING THE GUILTY – God is the Just Judge, He is Justice, He is a Jealous God; God chastens believers and judges the unrighteous who hate Him and walk in iniquity. Again, note this in context of the 10 commandments (2nd commandment); you shall not make or carve an image, making for yourself an idol to worship (Exo. 20:4-6).

"...The Lord, the Lord God (Jehovah = "the existing One") merciful and gracious, longsuffering and abounding in goodness and truth, keeping mercy for thousands, forgiving iniquity and transgression and sin, by no means clearing the guilty, visiting the iniquity of the fathers upon the children and the children's children to the third and the fourth generation." (Ex. 34:5-7)

ENCOUNTER GOD: FIRST, read Ex. 34:1-9 over slowly; then read the text above. **SECOND,** close your eyes, Go to God, PRAY for the Holy Spirit to teach you all things, PRAY for Holy Spirit to guide you into the Truth. **THIRD,** say the scripture slowly pausing for God to reveal Himself—to reveal TRUTH. **FOURTH,** answer the questions accordingly. REMEMBER talk to God, not just about Him.

UP – What does this verse show me about who You (God) are?

IN – What does this verse show me about what You (God) think about me?

OUT - How then shall I pray for my neighbor?

"...His name will be called Wonderful, Counselor, Mighty God, Everlasting Father…" (Isa. 9:6)

WE EACH RUN OUR OWN RACE OF HOLINESS (looking unto Jesus displaying the Father)

Read Hebrews 12:1-17 - From the beginning God has a Father's heart. Jesus revealed the nature of God as a Father who longs for intimacy with His family. Today, The Father's heart yearns to have a family who voluntarily loves Him and His Son (Bridegroom); God is a great King, BUT above all He is your Eternal Father (Isa. 9:6).

THE FATHER IS HOLY AND GOOD

Holy and Good: He is Creator, Majestic, & He is holy; sin cannot dwell before Him, BUT He made a way for you to be with Him—to live HOLY—through Jesus. Luke 15:11-32 the prodigal son 1st repented before the Holy Heavenly Father; 2nd the Father released a warm hug. Today, live holy repenting before the Holy Heavenly Father and then receive the Mercy and Grace—Fathers embrace.

Our Father is Holy and Good: Around the Throne of God the angels worship God with names of respect and adoration, for example, "To Him who sits upon the Throne, who lives forever and ever". Jesus made a startling declaration, when you pray say, "Our

Father". Today, you are not to stand at a distance from Him (Matt. 6:9); you pray to a Father that loves you.

Jesus is revealing the Father: Jesus reveals many facets of God's name and personality. Yet, God's Fatherhood comes to the forefront and dominates Jesus' revelation of what God is like (John 17:26). ***Today***, *The Father is still inviting you to search out who He is—be holy for I am holy.*

Sons and daughters: For eternity, you are the blessed of the Father. Satan says you are cursed and accused by the Father. You inherit the Kingdom prepared for you from the foundation of the world. The Father was thinking of you when He prepared the foundations of the world (Mt. 25:31-34). ***Today***, *you can fully walk in the affections and authority of a child of God—a New Creation. Your earthly father may not have left you a financial or spiritual inheritance; BUT GOD has a rich treasure for you!!*

Father calls us to be holy: Paul taught (2 Cor. 6:11 - Cor. 7:1), "Therefore, having these promises, beloved, let us cleanse ourselves from all filthiness of the flesh and spirit, perfecting holiness in the fear of God." He taught the church at Corinth to know and understand the Holy. Then, you freely enjoy the loving Father and walk in His inheritance towards you. ***Today***, *it is important to note that God loves you, but your sin keeps you from experiencing it freely; His love for you wars against sin.*

Adopting Abba Father: life is broken and unsettled until you know the embrace of the Adopting Father (Rom. 8:12-17). Human intimacy will not answer the deepest cry of your spirit; you're created to long for the touch of a father. ***Today***, *your primary emotional need is the assurance that you are enjoyed by The Father in your weakness; Firstly, you need revelation that the Father longs for you and enjoys you.*

For in You the fatherless finds mercy: The answer to your crisis of not having a father figure is found in God the Father; earthly parents point to your Heavenly Father. (Hos. 14:3). ***Today***, *you can live holy as you allow the Father to be your father and free your earthly parents from past pain.*

Luke 15 Father lost a son (and got Him back again): the story is not just about the son, but about a Father that is patient. The younger son asks for his inheritance, which was a great insult to a father. The father gave his son the money because he knew the heart of that son. He knew that his son would never come into intimacy with him until he was broken by the discovery of his sin and emptiness. ***Today***, *you live holy as you understand your sin and need for a patient saving Father* (Luke 15:11-32).

"...His name will be called Wonderful, Counselor, Mighty God, Everlasting Father..." (Isa. 9:6)

ENCOUNTER GOD: FIRST, read Isa. 9:1-7; then read the above scripture slowly. **SECOND,** close your eyes, Go to God, PRAY for the Holy Spirit to teach you all things, PRAY for Holy Spirit to guide you into the Truth. **THIRD,** say the scripture slowly pausing for God to reveal Himself—to reveal TRUTH. **FOURTH,** answer the questions accordingly. REMEMBER talk to God, not just about Him.

UP – What does this verse show me about who You (God) are?

IN – What does this verse show me about what You (God) think about me?

OUT - How then shall I pray for my neighbor?

"In this manner, therefore, pray: Our Father in heaven, Hallowed (Holy/Sacred) be Your name. Your kingdom come. Your will be done on earth as it is in heaven. Give us this day our daily bread. And forgive us our debts, As we forgive our debtors. And do not lead us into temptation, But deliver us from the evil one. For Yours is the kingdom and the power and the glory forever. Amen." (Matt. 6:9-13)

THE FATHER IS HOLY AND MADE YOU HOLY

HOLY FATHER MADE YOU FOR HOLINESS: The Father's Name, which describes His character (Firm Foundations #19), clearly describes who God is and what He thinks and feels about you. He is Holy, Glorious, Majestic, Awesome, Supreme Pleasure, Supreme Knowledge, Supreme Authority, AND Father made you for holiness. Our Father made a way for you to be Holy; He gave His Mercy to Wash you clean and Grace to empower you. He created you to succeed—to "be holy for I am Holy".

OUR FATHER IN HEAVEN: This is a prayer that Jesus taught you to Pray. Have you ever thought why He taught us to pray this way? This is the perfect prayer to produce PEACE in your life and the lives of those around you, AND this prayer will bring you revelation of God that will compel you to vigorously march forth in victorious holiness.

OUR FATHER IN HEAVEN, HALLOWED BE YOUR NAME: He is LOVE & HOLY. LOVE: the Perfect Patient Papa. He dwells in Heaven—loves you—and sent His Son to make you a child of God (w/eternal benefits package). He is HOLY, which declares the Fear of the Lord, and His name (see Firm Foundations #19) describes His nature and affections. Today, pray to your Father in Heaven and declare His holy nature into your life; minister His name back to Him and believe the character of His name will grow in you—making you holy as He is holy (1 Jn. 4:15-16).

YOUR KINGDOM COME: God is a King (see Ps. 2 & Firm Foundation #24), and He will dwell on a Throne in Jerusalem. Today, pray for His [King]dom to come freeing yourself from the kingdoms of this world (1 Jn. 2:15).

YOUR WILL BE DONE: God has a will (what He wants to accomplish). His will can be for today and tomorrow. Today, pray for His will in your life and that you will line up with His plan, freeing you from the frustration of doing things outside of His will. Remember, lay up your treasure in heaven (Matt. 6:19-21).

GIVE US THIS DAY OUR DAILY BREAD: The Good Father owns the cattle on 1000 hills (& owns the hill itself Ps. 50) and He is on your side—God brings provision for the vision. Today, STOP, give your heart and money to HIM in prayer, ask Him what He wills and pray for Him to provide. Remember, Mammon hates you & seeks to destroy, BUT God provides (Matt. 6:24)

FORGIVE US OUR DEBTS, AS WE FORGIVE OUR DEBTORS: God is a loving, merciful Father with the power, and desire, to forgive your sin. **DEBTS:** you and our nation have sin stacked up against us and it is important to ask forgiveness. **FORGIVE:** you have the power to forgive others, which frees you from the pain of the past, allowing your heart to be holy as He is Holy (forgiving someone of what they did means turning them over to Jesus the Just Judge, allowing Him to take your case and administer justice as He wills). *Today, pray to become like God, and forgive those who have sinned against you. Remember, "For if you forgive men their trespasses, your heavenly Father will also forgive you. But if you do not forgive men their trespasses, neither will your Father forgive your trespasses."* (Matt. 6:14-15)

DO NOT LEAD US INTO TEMPTATION, BUT DELIVER US: God the Father is the perfect leader. God does not tempt you. Instead, you are drawn away by evil desire inside you (Jas. 1:12-18). Today, pray for God to lead you away from temptation; you are turning away from your own ways and choosing to turn towards Him.

YOURS IS THE KINGDOM AND THE POWER AND THE GLORY FOREVER: God has a plan(s) for you that are eternal. *Today, pray this verse—don't worry— BELIEVE He holds tomorrow (Matt. 6:25-34) And in life's storms build your life upon the never-ending ROCK, who is Christ (Matt. 7:24-29).*

"In this manner, therefore, pray: Our Father in heaven, Hallowed be Your name. Your kingdom come. Your will be done on earth as it is in heaven. Give us this day our daily bread. And forgive us our debts, As we forgive our debtors. And do not lead us into temptation, But deliver us from the evil one. For Yours is the kingdom and the power and the glory forever. Amen." (Matt. 6:9-13)

ENCOUNTER GOD: FIRST, read Matt. 6:5-15; then read the above scripture (Matt. 6:9-13) over slowly. **SECOND,** close your eyes, Go to God, PRAY for the Holy Spirit to teach you all things, PRAY the Holy Spirit guide you into the Truth. **THIRD,** say the scripture slowly pausing for God to reveal Himself—to highlight a section of the Scripture. **FOURTH,** answer the questions accordingly. REMEMBER talk to God, not just about Him.

UP – (**BELIEVE**) What does this verse show me about who You (God) are?

IN – (**BELIEVE; OBEY**) What does this verse show me about what You (God) think about me?

OUT - How then shall I pray for my neighbor?

ordinary people called to do extraordinary things

"…Let all bitterness, wrath, anger, clamor, and evil speaking be put away from you, with all malice. And be kind to one another, tenderhearted, forgiving one another, even as God in Christ forgave you." (Eph. 4:31-32)

The truth about forgiveness and the consequences of not forgiving others:
God is Holy (He forgives and so must you) – God is Holy and you are called to be just like Him; He forgives you; therefore, you must forgive others. God told Moses He was "The Lord, the Lord God, merciful and gracious, longsuffering, and abounding in goodness and truth, keeping mercy for thousands, forgiving iniquity and transgression and sin (Exo. 34:5-7).

God grants forgiveness – God wants to bring you forgiveness! God wants an eternal relationship with you; He delights in Mercy not sacrifice (Micah 7:18)! If you sin, God does not want you trapped in your sin; instead He wants you to repent, washing you clean in His Mercy (Loving-Kindness). **Old Testament** - when you sinned, you would bring your sin offering before a priest and they would make atonement for you. **New Testament** – when you sin, Jesus is the sacrifice, His blood acquits and redeems you. Therefore, Jesus is the perfect Priest and sacrifice that brings you to the Father for atonement, and then Father FORGIVES you and washes you in Mercy.

You must forgive others – Jesus taught us to pray for forgiveness and shared the consequences of not forgiving others. He said, "And forgive us our debts, As we forgive our debtors…"For if you forgive men their trespasses, your heavenly Father will also forgive you. But if you do not forgive men their trespasses, neither will your Father forgive your trespasses" (Matt. 6:12-15).

Dealing with those that sin against you – **(1)** "…go and tell him his fault between you and him alone. If he hears you, you have gained your brother **(2)** But if he will not hear, take with you one or two more, that 'by the mouth of two or three witnesses every word may be established.'**(3)** And if he refuses to hear them, tell it to the church. **(4)** But if he refuses even to hear the church, let him be to you like a heathen and a tax collector (Matt. 18:15-19). The prayer for "binding and loosing" (verse 19) should be understood in context of Christian unity; Christian unity is linked to your forgiving correctly.

Consequences if you don't forgive – Jesus had compassion on you and forgave you, "Then the master of that servant was moved with compassion, released him, and forgave him the debt." You must also forgive those that are indebted to you (who have done you wrong) or you will be thrown into living torment until you can repay (Matt. 18:21-35). You have a "ministry of reconciliation" (2 Cor. 5:16-21).

Pray for forgiveness – God calls you to ask or "pray" for forgiveness from sin; personal and corporate life"…if My people who are called by My name will humble themselves, and pray and seek My face, and turn from their wicked ways, then I will hear from heaven, and will forgive their sin and heal their land" (2 Chron. 7:14; Dan. 9:19; Joel 2:12-17; Amos 7:2; Matt. 6:5-15; Matt. 11:25).

Forgiveness vs. justice – Forgiveness is not giving up your Justice. When you forgive someone, you're giving the pain to God and asking Him, the Just Fair Judge, to bring Heavenly Justice, which will be a merciful and Just Judgment; God desires that none would perish, but all would come to repentance (2 Pt. 3:9). Asking forgiveness and forgiving another allows God's love to grow in you (Lu. 7:47).

How to get forgiveness from God (Questions: what do you need forgiveness from?)

1. **Repent** – **(1)** Tell God you are sorry **(2)** you are wrong **(3)** you don't want to do it again.
2. **Change** – ask Him how you can change your ways; "worthy of repentance" (Lu. 3:8)

How to forgive another: (Questions: Who do you need to forgive? Maybe write a list out.)

1. **Talk to God** – dialogue with God, ask Him to expose anything in your heart.
2. **Matthew 18** – go to a brother or sister that has hurt you and follow the Matt.18 path (see above).
3. **Forgive them** – make sure to forgive them face-to-face, where you verbally say "I forgive you for _____" (do not go face-to-face if your life's in danger, or the situation is to painful; Instead, write a letter).
4. **"Love your enemies, bless those who curse you, do good to those who hate you, and pray for those who spitefully use you and persecute you"** (Matt. 5:43-45).
5. **Ask them to forgive you** – this is crucial to a healthy community and John 17 unity.

"...Let all bitterness, wrath, anger, clamor, and evil speaking be put away from you, with all malice. And be kind to one another, tenderhearted, forgiving one another, <u>even as God in Christ forgave you</u>." (Eph. 4:31-32)

ENCOUNTER GOD: FIRST, read Eph.4:25-32; then read the above underlined scripture over slowly. **SECOND,** close your eyes, Go to God, PRAY for the Holy Spirit to teach you all things, PRAY for Holy Spirit to guide you into the Truth. **THIRD,** say the scripture slowly pausing FOR GOD TO REVEAL HIMSELF—to reveal TRUTH. **FOURTH,** answer the questions accordingly. REMEMBER TALK TO GOD, NOT JUST ABOUT HIM.

UP – What does this verse show me about who You (God) are?

IN – What does this verse show me about what You (God) think about me?

OUT - How then shall I pray for my neighbor?

ordinary people called to do extraordinary things

"...Therefore we also, since we are surrounded by so great a cloud of witnesses, let us lay aside every weight, and the sin which so easily ensnares us, and let us run with endurance the race that is set before us, looking unto Jesus, the author and finisher of our faith, who for the joy that was set before Him endured the cross, despising the shame, and has sat down at the right hand of the throne of God". (Heb. 12:1-2)

WE EACH RUN OUR OWN RACE OF HOLINESS (looking unto Jesus)

You are a child of God and the Bride of Christ, and you are called to run your own race. God's ultimate eternal purpose for creation is to provide a family for Himself including faithful children for Himself, and an equally yoked Bride for Jesus as His eternal companion (non-sexual). God promised to give Jesus an inheritance consisting of a people whom He fully possesses in love. I [the Father] will give You [Jesus] the nations for Your inheritance, and the ends of the earth for Your possession. (Ps. 2:8)

HEBREWS 12 CALLS US TO RUN THE RACE OF HOLINESS:

JESUS: You run your own race of holiness with others, but the chief way that you get there is by looking at Jesus, which means you search out His life on a daily basis. Jesus ran His race because He looked to the joy of future glory with the family of God (John 17:21-23) and so can you. He calls you to run with: oil of intimacy (or the 1st commandment 1st place in your life); (Matt. 25:1-13) and to be faithful, walking with grace according to your talents given by God (Matt. 25:14-30); and work acts of justice according to the measure and standard of the Just Judge (Matt. 25:31-46).

Heb. 12:1-2: *"Therefore we also, since we are surrounded by so great a cloud of witnesses, let us lay aside every weight, and the sin which so easily ensnares us, and let us run with endurance the race that is set before us…"* Therefore, the writer is calling for faithfulness, unto holiness, in your full life's race, according to God's personal call on your life. Cloud of witnesses: you can live holy because those that went before you (and are cheering you on now) also lived holy lives; lay aside: you are invited to walk free from sin and brokenness because of those that have gone before did. Run with endurance: your life's race is at a marathon pace, not a sprint.

THE DISCIPLINE OF GOD (Heb. 12:3-11)

a. **Consider Him:** Jesus was verbally and physically attacked and He persevered; ***Today***, *pray to overcome personal attacks and walk in holiness because Jesus did.*

b. **You have not yet resisted to bloodshed, striving against sin:** Jesus sweat drops like blood, in the place of prayer, to do the Father's will (Lu. 22:44); Question: is God's grace stronger than your sinful flesh? ***Today,*** *pray to access the same GRACE to persevere against sin.*

c. **Chastening:** God is a holy and just Father who chastens (instructs and trains us into righteousness); ***Today,*** *God wants to train and instruct you, and you need to respond accordingly;* **Positive:** You say yes to the correction; walk away from sin; say yes to God's leadership. **Negative:** whine, complain, and give excuses as to why you can continue in sin.

d. **Holiness:** A loving Father chastens, and it is the way to correction; if you endure the chastening then you have the inheritance of children of God—in holiness. ***Today,*** *thank God for His Fatherly correction—cooperate with His chastening—invite GRACE to overcome your struggling sin.*

SPIRITUAL RENEWAL (Hebrews 12:12-17): "strengthen the hands which hang down, and the feeble knees, and make straight paths for your feet, so that what is lame may not be dislocated"; You are called to your individual race of holiness; how you run will affect the corporate body; ***Today,*** *ask God to give you a higher vision to live a holy life, which means you will see "HIS PLAN".*

"and let us run with endurance the race that is set before us, looking unto Jesus, the author and finisher of our faith, who for the joy that was set before Him endured the cross, despising the shame, and has sat down at the right hand of the throne of God." (Heb. 12:1-2)

ENCOUNTER GOD: FIRST, read Heb. 12:1-17; then read above underlined scripture over slowly. **SECOND,** close your eyes, Go to God, PRAY for the Holy Spirit to teach you all things, PRAY for Holy Spirit to guide you into the Truth. **THIRD,** say the scripture slowly pausing FOR GOD TO REVEAL HIMSELF—to reveal TRUTH. **FOURTH,** answer the questions accordingly. REMEMBER TALK TO GOD, NOT JUST ABOUT HIM.

UP – What does this verse show me about who You (God) are?

IN – What does this verse show me about what You (God) think about me?

OUT - How then shall I pray for my neighbor?

"…The kingdom of heaven is like a certain <u>king</u> who arranged a <u>marriage for his son</u>, and sent out his servants to call those who were <u>invited to the wedding</u>…"
(Matt. 22:2-3)

WHAT DOES THE BIBLE SAY ABOUT JESUS' IDENTITY BEFORE HE RETURNS?

Positive and Negative: In the years leading up to Jesus' return, you will see a unique time period, both positive and negative. Positive: The greatest outpouring of the Spirit in history is coming, which will be greater than the book of Acts in power (Acts 2:17-21). The Gospel of the Kingdom will be preached in the entire world as a witness ([Mt. 24:14](Mt. 24:14)). As the light gets brighter, the darkness will get darker. Negative: satan will rage against the human race and God's most severe judgments will be poured out against the Antichrist's empire ([Mt. 24:21-22](Mt. 24:21-22)).

BRIDEGROOM. JUDGE. KING: The Word and the Spirit, added together, give understanding. They declare Jesus as Bridegroom, King, and Judge at the end of the age. As the <u>Bridegroom</u>, He is filled with <u>desire</u> for His people. As <u>King</u>, He possesses all <u>power</u>. As <u>Judge</u>, He is zealous to administer righteous Justice and removing all that hinders love, as He confronts oppression. In Jesus' last message before the upper room discourse ([Jn. 14:17](Jn. 14:17)), He revealed Himself as Bridegroom, King, and Judge ([Mt. 25:31-46](Mt. 25:31-46)).

JESUS BELOVED BRIDEGROOM: Jesus is revealed as the One with holy passionate love for you. In Jesus' last public message to Israel, He emphasized the revelation of God as Bridegroom, King, and Judge (Mt. 22:1-14). Later in that same chapter He further emphasizes His love for us and our love towards Him, ourselves, and others; Today, the Holy Spirit is restoring the first commandment to first place in your life and the church (Matt. 22:34-40).

SOVEREIGN KING: Jesus is revealed as the One KING who possesses all power and authority. As THE KING, Jesus restores individual lives, all the nations, and the earth (atmosphere, agriculture, animals, etc.). ***Today***, *you are invited to walk holy because you are a servant of a Righteous KING. Therefore, when you know Him as King, you will experience the supernatural power of God your life and ministry* (Ps. 2:6; Isa. 2:1-4; Matt. 22:2-3; Rev. 17:14).

RIGHTEOUS JUDGE: Jesus is revealed as the One JUDGE who is righteous in His JUSTICE; He had great zeal to intervene and remove everything that stops His love from coming to you; Jesus confronts all rebellion and brokenness instead of ignoring it (Zech. 1:14; 8:2; Ezek. 38:18-19; Rev. 19:2). Jesus is the only man worthy to judge the nations because, as Creator, He understands the design of the human spirit, and because He humbled Himself to become a man (2 Cor. 8:9).

You prepare your heart to live HOLY today—affecting tomorrow: The Father gives understanding about Jesus' identity, before the second coming, so that you can overcome and live righteous today and prepare the generation that will witness His return.

²True and righteous are His judgments, because He has judged the great harlot who corrupted the earth with her fornication; and He has avenged on her the blood of His servants shed by her…⁷Give Him glory, for the marriage of the Lamb has come, and His wife has made herself ready…⁹Blessed are those who are called to the marriage supper of the Lamb! …¹¹In righteousness He judges and makes war…¹⁵He should strike the nations. He Himself will rule them…He Himself treads the winepress of…the wrath of Almighty God…¹⁶on His thigh a name written: **KING OF KINGS** *and* LORD OF LORDS. (Rev. 19:2-16) & (Rev. 21:2-11)

ordinary people called to do extraordinary things

"...The kingdom of heaven is like a certain <u>king</u> who arranged a <u>marriage for his son</u>, ³and sent out his servants to call those who were <u>invited to the wedding</u>..." (Matt. 22:2-3)

ENCOUNTER GOD: FIRST, read Matt. 22:1-14; then read above underlined scripture over slowly. **SECOND,** close your eyes, Go to God, PRAY for the Holy Spirit to teach you all things, PRAY for Holy Spirit to guide you into the Truth. **THIRD,** say the scripture slowly pausing FOR GOD TO REVEAL HIMSELF—to reveal TRUTH. **FOURTH,** answer the questions accordingly. REMEMBER TALK TO GOD, NOT JUST ABOUT HIM.

UP – What does this verse show me about who You (God) are?

IN – What does this verse show me about what You (God) think about me?

OUT - How then shall I pray for my neighbor?

BIBLIOGRAPHY

Books:

(2) Mac, Toby and Tait, Michael in Association with Wall Builders (2004).
   Under God (page 16). Bloomington, Minnesota: Bethany House Publishers

Website(s):

Biblegateway, (since 1993); retrieved January 2018 from https://www.biblegateway.com/

Bickle, Mike (since 2008); retrieved January 2018 from https://mikebickle.org/

(1) Billy Graham's Evangelical Association (March 26, 2014); Billy Graham's Answer: What is Sin? Are All Sins Equal in God's Eyes?

(3) Snow, Shane (August 17, 2010); "The Rise of Texting"; https://mashable.com/2010/08/17/text-messaging-infographic/#RW3qIAGTUmqB

(4) The Nielsen Company (October 14, 2010) U.S. TEEN MOBILE REPORT CALLING YESTERDAY, TEXTING TODAY, USING APPS TOMORROW

NOW WHAT?

Now that you have finished going through Firm Foundations what is next? Did you know the bible says:

"Go therefore and make disciples of all the nations, baptizing them in the name of the Father and of the Son and of the Holy Spirit." (Matt. 28:19)

So, what is your plan to "GO" and make disciples? I think you are the answer to this bible verse. You are an ordinary person called to do and extraordinary things. Why not take this manual and start a group—today? This does not have to be complicated.

It can be a:

- Youth and young adults
- College and university students
- Market place
- Prison
- Homeless
- Church or home group
- In a mall!!

We want to help you get there. Check out holyclubs.com for "starting a group"!!

Now go and run your own race…

        At your own pace…

    And you will end up, at just the right place…

            Near to God's comforting face…

www.ingramcontent.com/pod-product-compliance
Lightning Source LLC
Chambersburg PA
CBHW041521220426
43669CB00002B/17